Spotlight on Young Children

Supporting
Dual Language Learners

Meghan Dombrink-Green and **Holly Bohart,** editors
With **Karen N. Nemeth**

National Association for the Education of Young Children
Washington, DC

National Association for the
Education of Young Children
1401 H Street NW, Suite 600
Washington, DC 20005
202-232-8777 • 800-424-2460
www.naeyc.org

NAEYC Publishing

Chief Publishing Officer
Derry Koralek

Editor-in-Chief
Kathy Charner

Director of Creative Services
Edwin C. Malstrom

Managing Editor
Mary Jaffe

Senior Editor
Holly Bohart

Senior Graphic Designer
Malini Dominey

Associate Editor
Meghan Dombrink-Green

Associate Editor
Elizabeth Wegner

Editorial Assistant
Ryan Smith

Through its publications
program, the National
Association for the Education
of Young Children (NAEYC)
provides a forum for discussion of major issues and
ideas in the early childhood
field, with the hope of provok-
ing thought and promoting
professional growth. The
views expressed or implied in
this book are not necessarily
those of the Association or
its members.

The following are selections published previously in *Young Children* and the
issues in which they appeared: J. Youngquist and B. Martínez-Griego,
"Learning in English, Learning in Spanish: A Head Start Program Changes Its
Approach," July 2009; K. Nemeth and P. Brillante, "Solving the Puzzle: Dual
Language Learners With Challenging Behaviors," July 2011; K.N. Nemeth and
V. Erdosi, "Enhancing Practice With Infants and Toddlers From Diverse Lan-
guage and Cultural Backgrounds," September 2012; I. Alanís, "Where's Your
Partner? Pairing Bilingual Learners in Preschool and Primary Grade Dual
Language Classrooms," March 2013; M.K. Jones and P.L. Shue, "Engaging Pre-
kindergarten Dual Language Learners in Projects," March 2013; E.S. Magruder,
W.W. Hayslip, L.M. Espinosa, and C. Matera, "Many Languages, One Teacher:
Supporting Language and Literacy Development for Preschool Dual Language
Learners," March 2013; D.R. Meier, "Integrating Content and Mechanics in
New Language Learners' Writing in the Primary Classroom," March 2013;
K.N. Nemeth and F.S. Simon, "Using Technology as a Teaching Tool for Dual
Language Learners in Preschool Through Grade 3," March 2013.

Permissions

The article *Integrating Content and Mechanics in New Language Learners'
Writing* on pages 71–78 is adapted, with permission, from Daniel R. Meier,
Teaching Children to Write: Constructing Meaning and Mastering Mechanics
(New York: Teachers College Press, 2011).

Photo Credits

Courtesy of article authors: iv (top, bottom), 16, 19, 22, 51, 53, 54, 61, 62, 79
(top and bottom), 82, 83, 84

Courtesy of United Way Center for Excellence in Early Education: iv (third
from the top), 65, 67, 69

Copyright © Peg Callaghan: cover (top right) 46; Bob Ebbesen: iii (second
from the bottom), 33, 39; Julia Luckenbill: iii (top, second from the top,
third from the top), 1, 5, 13, 23; NAEYC: iii (third from the bottom), 24, 29;
Elisabeth Nichols: cover (bottom right), iv (second from the top), 35, 58;
Marilyn Nolt: iii (bottom), 43, 45; Jude Keith Rose: 7; Ellen B. Senisi:
cover (left), iv (second from the bottom), 11, 27, 31, 71, 77; Susan Woog
Wagner/© NAEYC: 15, 47

Spotlight on Young Children: Supporting Dual Language Learners.

Library of Congress Control Number: 2014951934

ISBN: 978-1-938113-13-0

Item 2210

Contents

Karen N. Nemeth

Introduction

Mr. Garber waved and said "auf Wiedersehen" to Marco, the last child to be picked up from his kindergarten classroom that day. He enjoyed working with younger children after years of teaching students in fifth grade. When he walked into the staff room for the afternoon meeting, the other teachers asked how his new dual language learner was doing. "Marco is doing fine," said Mr. Garber. "But I guess he's actually a triple language learner. His family is from Cuba, but he grew up in Germany and now he is also learning English!"

Dual language learners (DLLs) are young children who are growing up with two or more languages. NAEYC follows the Office of Head Start's definition of dual language learners as children who "are learning two (or more) languages at the same time, as well as those learning a second language while continuing to develop their first (or home) language. The term *dual language learners* encompasses other terms frequently used, such as Limited English Proficient (LEP), bilingual, English language learners (ELL), English learners, and children who speak a Language Other Than English (LOTE)" (2008, 1).

About 25 percent of children younger than 18 in the United States live with at least one parent who is an immigrant (Nwosu, Batalova, & Auclair 2014). This means that many early childhood educators will work with children and families who speak a language other than English.

Young dual language learners are building skills in a second language while developing skills in their home language. Thus, their learning needs differ from those of their peers who speak one language and older children who learn a second language after fully developing their first.

The term *dual language learners* reflects DLLs' need for support in learning both of their languages. Children need support of their home language to access the prior knowledge they have built up in that language, and a strong foundation in the home language makes it easier for children to learn English (Genesee 2010). As the contributing authors in this book explain, helping young children grow and learn with two or more languages should focus on conversations and meaningful interactions. Iliana Alanís, in her article "Where's Your Partner? Pairing Bilingual Learners in Dual Language Classrooms," notes that "to develop a first or second language, children need to hear language in rich and meaningful contexts that help them connect what they are learning with their prior experiences."

Woven throughout the articles is the importance of engaging families of dual language learners in the early childhood program. In "Principles for Leading a Dual Language Program," authors Paula Moujalli, Laura Haim, and Ryan Pontier note that "families feel comfortable when they can communicate with their children's teachers and when they know those professionals will nurture their children's ability to communicate using two languages." Respecting all families and their home languages supports children's self-esteem and helps strengthen family bonds. It is also important for children to see their home languages and cultures reflected in the materials, displays, and practices in their programs to help them feel valued and important.

This collection of articles supports educators and administrators of programs that serve dual language learners from birth through age 8 and their families. The articles provide information about DLLs' language and literacy development and share specific recommendations that can be implemented in all programs. The practical, evidence-based strategies discussed will prepare early childhood professionals to meet the educational needs of dual language learners and their families.

Rebecca Parlakian and Jennifer Frey, in "Creating Supportive Caregiving Environments for Infant and Toddler Dual Language Learners," suggest five areas in which programs can provide high-quality language environments to support very young DLLs and their families.

A well-established, diverse infant/toddler program provides the foundation for Karen N. Nemeth and Valeria Erdosi's "Enhancing Practice With Infants and Toddlers From Diverse Language and Cultural Backgrounds." The authors suggest strategies for adapting the environment and involving families to support infants' and toddlers' home languages and cultures.

In "Many Languages, One Teacher: Supporting Language and Literacy Development for Dual Language Learners," Elizabeth S. Magruder, Whitcomb W. Hayslip, Linda M. Espinosa, and Carola Matera describe the challenges of meeting the diverse language needs of young children. They explain intentional plans and techniques for supporting preschoolers' home language learning while facilitating their English language learning.

In "Learning in English, Learning in Spanish: A Head Start Program Changes Its Approach," Joan Youngquist and Bárbara Martínez-Griego detail the story of a Head Start program's journey to transform its approach to language and learning—from reflecting on program policies and practices for teaching preschool DLLs to making significant, exciting changes that more fully support children's learning.

Many teachers find it difficult to determine if a child's challenging behavior is due to a language difference or a developmental issue. In "Supporting Dual Language Learners With Challenging Behaviors," Karen N. Nemeth and Pamela Brillante identify possible causes of and solutions to the challenging behaviors of preschoolers who are DLLs.

In "Engaging Dual Language Learners in Projects," Meredith K. Jones and Pamela L. Shue explain how in-depth projects in a preschool setting encourage peer-to-peer communication and build vocabulary and social skills in all children.

Iliana Alanís describes strategies for pairing children that help them learn academic concepts and develop language skills through natural conversation. The easy-to-implement suggestions in "Where's Your Partner? Pairing Bilingual Learners in Dual Language Classrooms" can be used with children in preschool through third grade.

In "Using Technology as a Teaching Tool for Dual Language Learners," Karen N. Nemeth and Fran S. Simon describe ways to choose and use a variety of technology tools to support DLLs in preschool through third grade.

Teaching writing skills to dual language learners in kindergarten through third grade is the topic of Daniel R. Meier's "Integrating Content and Mechanics in New Language Learners' Writing." He emphasizes the role of oral language development in building children's writing skills.

Administrators and directors of early childhood programs will find guidance for implementing a dual language program in "Principles for Leading a Dual Language Program." Authors Paula Moujalli, Laura Haim, and Ryan W. Pontier offer suggestions for supporting children, families, and staff in programs serving infants through preschoolers.

Karen N. Nemeth, EdM, is an author and consultant who specializes in supporting early learning for children who speak two or more languages.

Each article in this collection includes two special features: Engaging Families and Challenging Common Myths About DLLs. Each **Engaging Families** feature offers a real-life story illustrating how early childhood programs and families of dual language learners partner to provide rich environments for children's learning. The **Challenging Common Myths About DLLs** feature gives key research findings on dual language learners, helping educators understand the strengths and needs of young DLLs and implications for the learning environment. The findings, edited by Karen Nemeth, are from *PreK–3rd: Challenging Common Myths About Dual Language Learners: An Update to the Seminal 2008 Report,* by Linda M. Espinosa, PreK–3rd Policy to Action Brief No. Ten, Foundation for Child Development, August 2013. It can be located at http://fcd-us.org/sites/default/files/Challenging%20Common%20Myths%20Update.pdf. The page number in each Challenging Common Myths About DLLs box refers to the page in the report where more details can be found.

The book closes with a study guide by Karen N. Nemeth that poses questions to expand on the content of each article. Readers can reflect on the questions alone, talk about them with colleagues, or discuss them as participants in a class or workshop led by a facilitator. The guide begins with "Recalling Your Own Early Experiences," which asks readers to think about their own language and literacy experiences. The section "Expanding on Each Article" includes a brief summary of each article and specific questions and follow-up activities. In the last section of the study guide, "Making Connections," readers consider the big picture, examine their curricula and ways to improve their teaching practices, plan ways to involve families, and identify next steps.

References

Genesee, F. 2010. "Dual Language Development in Preschool Children." Chap. 4 in *Young English Language Learners: Current Research and Emerging Directions for Practice and Policy,* eds. E.E. García & E.C. Frede, 59–79. New York: Teachers College Press.

Nwosu, C., J. Batalova, & G. Auclair. 2014. "Frequently Requested Statistics on Immigrants and Immigration in the United States." Migration Policy Institute. www.migrationpolicy.org/article/frequently-requested-statistics-immigrants-and-immigration-united-states/#7.

Office of Head Start. 2008. *Dual Language Learning: What Does It Take? Head Start Dual Language Report.* Washington, DC: Office of Head Start. https://eclkc.ohs.acf.hhs.gov/hslc/tta-system/teaching/eecd/Dual%20 Language%20Learners%20and%20Their%20Families/Learning%20in%20Two%20Languages/DLANA_ final_2009%5B1%5D.pdf.

On the opening page of the articles, this logo and the numbers indicate which of the 10 NAEYC Early Childhood Program Standards the articles address. This information guides programs for young children ages birth through kindergarten seeking NAEYC Accreditation or improving program quality.

naeyc® 2,3

Rebecca
Parlakian and
Jennifer Frey

naeyc® 2, 3

Creating Supportive Caregiving Environments for Infant and Toddler Dual Language Learners

The process of learning to communicate begins at birth and is increasingly taking place in more than one language for many infants and toddlers. Young children who are "acquiring two languages simultaneously or who are developing their primary language as they learn a second language" are considered to be dual language learners (DLLs) (Gutiérrez, Zepeda, & Castro 2010, 334). These languages are typically introduced from birth, although exposure to each language varies based on children's individual experiences and family practices.

Dual Language Learning From Birth to Three

Dual language learning may actually begin in the womb, as babies are exposed to the sounds and cadences of the languages spoken by those around them. Newborns, in fact, prefer languages that are rhythmically similar to the ones they hear before birth (Klass 2011), and babies born to bilingual mothers prefer listening to both of the languages spoken by their mothers over other languages (Byers-Heinlein, Burns, & Werker 2010). Remarkably, these babies can distinguish between the two languages (as measured by the frequency of their suck on a rubber nipple; more frequent sucks are a measure of baby's interest in and recognition of novelty) (Byers-Heinlein, Burns, & Werker 2010).

It is widely accepted that, over time, infants learning two languages develop two "separate but connected linguistic systems" (Castro & Espinosa 2014, 35). Receptive language skills appear to emerge early, with infants as young as 10 to 13 months old recognizing familiar words in each of their languages—a milestone that occurs at the same time in monolingual infants (Vihman et al. 2007; Poulin-Dubois et al. 2011).

In fact, dual language learners reach other language milestones—babbling, speaking their first word, combining two words, and using a 50-word vocabulary—at about the same time as monolingual children (Petitto et al. 2002; Genesee 2003; Hoff et al. 2012). The research is very clear: Learning two languages does not cause confusion or delays in language development, and even for infants, there is no advantage to immersion in English-only programs (August & Shanahan 2006).

DLL toddlers learn words at the same rate as monolingual children, although the words are divided across two languages (Hoff et al. 2012). While this means that dual language learners tend to have smaller English vocabularies than other children of the same age, the number of words in their total vocabulary (home language and English combined) is almost identical to that of monolingual children.

Children learning more than one language gain the ability to name the same object or concept in both languages by about age one and a half (Genesee & Nicoladis 2007). More balanced exposure to both of a child's languages leads to an enhanced ability to name familiar objects in both languages (Poulin-Dubois et al. 2011).

The more language young children hear, the larger their vocabularies tend to be (Hart & Risley 1995). The rate of language development among DLL toddlers varies in direct relation to their relative amount of exposure to each language (Hoff et al. 2012). That is, bilingually developing toddlers who hear more English than Spanish generally have stronger English skills and weaker Spanish skills, and the opposite is true as well. Thus, rich, consistent exposure to both languages is an important goal for DLL infants and toddlers and their families.

Rebecca Parlakian, MA, is the director of Parenting Resources at ZERO TO THREE and has developed resources addressing aspects of infant/toddler development and program development, including the cultural implications of caregiving. She also teaches graduate courses at The George Washington University.

Jennifer Frey, PhD, is an assistant professor in the Department of Special Education and Disability Studies at The George Washington University. Dr. Frey's primary area of research is early language and social behavior assessment and intervention for young children with developmental delays and young children at risk due to poverty-related factors.

Authentic Partnerships: Aligning the Early Childhood Environment With Family Beliefs and Practices

In this section we discuss five areas in which infant/toddler programs can provide high-quality language environments to support very young dual language learners and their families: engagement with families, caregiving practices, the language environment, the physical environment, and supervision and professional development.

Relationship Building and Engaging With Families

Establishing authentic relationships with families—characterized by collaboration and mutual respect—is critical to supporting the healthy development of young dual language learners (and all children). It is likely that each family in the program will have a slightly different approach to supporting their children's bilingualism. Infant/toddler professionals need to be flexible, responsive, open, and collaborative when partnering with families. Learning more about families' strengths, resources, and expectations builds a bridge between home and program and helps teachers provide an environment that supports and is relevant to both children and families. Ideally, discussions with families begin before a child starts the program and continue throughout her involvement.

The U.S. Department of Health and Human Services (2014) offers suggestions for gathering background information when talking with families. It is helpful to ask questions that address **language background** ("What language(s) does your child speak?"); **dual language development** ("Did your child grow up with two languages from birth?"); **language dominance** ("When your child wants to communicate, which language does he use?"); **home language experiences** ("Who speaks the home language to her?"); **English language experiences** ("Who speaks English to him?"); and **individual child characteristics** ("What toys does your child especially like to play with?"). Discussing such questions can help families and professionals establish shared language and literacy goals for children and provide a framework for more active family engagement in the program as a whole.

During home visits teachers can learn more about families' languages and parenting practices. These visits contribute to a developing sense of trust and mutual respect between families and professionals and help teachers understand how best to support children. Meeting families in their community, and in their home, places explicit value on the family language and culture.

Engaging families in program activities is a critical part of supporting young dual language learners' development. Families might contribute recipes for cooking activities; share stories or sing songs with the children in their home language; or assist with translation of program information and newsletters. In addition, Nemeth (2012) notes a wide range of roles that parents can play in infant/toddler programs, including "play buddies" (adult volunteers who play with the children), "rockers and snugglers" (adult volunteers who help soothe babies to sleep), and "crafters" (adult volunteers who create displays or toys for the program). Teachers can record parents telling stories or sharing songs (with their permission and in accordance with program guidelines) and make these recordings part of rituals like naptime or include them in a toddler room book area. Programs can also offer experiences for parents themselves, like English as a Second Language classes or educational or recreational activities, such as groups for crafting or learning home repair skills. By creating these opportunities, programs open the door to parents—literally and figuratively.

Engaging Families

Anneliese-Maria started in the Threes room in October. Her mother is Swedish and her father is Peruvian, and Anneliese-Maria speaks both of her parents' languages. She was now immersed in a classroom where the primary language was English, and she did not speak a single word the entire year. Through regular meetings with her parents, we knew that she spoke nonstop at home, mostly in Spanish (the language used by both parents) and occasionally in Swedish (her second language). Despite our best efforts—including having her parents come to the classroom to share Spanish and Swedish songs and stories with the children, cooking foods from Anneliese-Maria's (and other children's) family recipes, hiring a Spanish-speaking assistant teacher, and scaffolding peer play to include Anneliese-Maria—she remained silent in the classroom. The following November, Anneliese-Maria finally spoke her first words at school. Slowly, over time, she joined the chorus of preschoolers' questions, stories, songs, and jokes.

Anneliese-Maria and her family taught me that development cannot be rushed; children take the time they need to feel comfortable, learn, and risk speaking in a new language. Creating a cross-cultural classroom will not unfold the same way in every situation, but it always begins with forging authentic relationships between families and staff and trusting children's individual development.

Enrollment materials and ongoing family communications should be translated, whenever possible, into the home languages of the families. Programs may also include a statement in their enrollment materials that explains their approach to serving DLL infants and toddlers and their families.

Caregiving Practices

Establishing a warm, trusting relationship with an infant or toddler is the first, and most important, step in supporting the child's development, regardless of language status. For very young dual language learners, this relationship offers a safe home base from which to learn and explore and a place of comfort and soothing as they navigate a new linguistic environment. Over time, primary caregivers become expert in interpreting children's unique cues, vocalizations, and early vocabulary, especially important for a dual language learner who may have difficulty communicating his needs.

An infant's day is often characterized by intimate, repeated routines—from feeding to diapering to naptime—that are shared with important caregiving adults. For infant/toddler professionals, "every interaction [they] have with a child is a cultural exchange" (Parlakian & Sánchez 2006, 56). Asking parents how these routines are performed at home and replicating them as much as possible at the program contributes to young children's sense of safety and security. Learning the words families use to describe key routines (e.g., how to say "naptime" or the word used for bottle or bowel movement) provides consistency between the home and the early childhood setting. (See p. 48 in this book for a list of "survival" words and phrases in English and Spanish.)

For example, how often are babies held at home? How are they held (on the parent's back, in a sling, in one's arms)? How are babies fed? Are toddlers fed by adults or do they feed themselves? Understanding the ways in which families care for children helps teachers understand what children expect when they enter the setting and gives teachers insight into a child's behavior. For example, a toddler may appear to be a picky eater because she is fed by an adult at home and is expecting a similar routine in the early childhood setting.

An important part of any early care and education program is engaging very young children in exploration and learning. With infant/toddler DLLs, it's best to introduce songs and classroom routines gradually and to use a lot of repetition. Keeping these routines consistent throughout the year lets children master them and become full contributors to the group.

To help toddlers understand what will happen next in the classroom schedule, consider using picture cards that show, for example, a photo of snack time or of the naptime cot labeled with simple descriptive words. Toddlers who have difficulty with transitions in a new linguistic environment may benefit from an individualized photo schedule with small photos of each routine throughout the day. For DLLs younger than 18 months, pair verbal language with more concrete props, such as holding out a diaper while saying, "Diaper time," or holding up a banana while announcing, "Time for snack. Let's eat a banana!"

Language Environment

Research indicates that teachers should focus on helping preschool dual language learners develop oral language skills in both languages while simultaneously building early literacy skills (Castro et al. 2011). Teachers of infants and toddlers can apply this guidance in a developmentally appropriate way by offering children numerous rich interactions in both languages and by providing literacy experiences (shared book reading, group reading, and other group time activities) that include texts and stories representative of families' cultures and languages.

Infant/toddler professionals can use children's home languages and English for different routines and activities throughout the day; for example, they might use English for group time and Spanish during playtime (Nemeth & Erdosi 2014). To provide rich exposure to both languages, programs can hire staff who speak children's home languages, engage volunteers from children's language communities, or identify college students majoring in children's home languages to assist in the program.

Monolingual teachers can learn key words, simple songs or rhymes, and commonly used phrases ("Time to go outside!") in the children's home languages. They can support young dual language learners' language and literacy skills through planned curricular activities that scaffold children's understanding and comprehension (Gillanders & Castro 2007). For example, before sharing a book, **identify a few core vocabulary words** from the text that are critical for comprehension of the storyline. For times when books are shared spontaneously with children, adults can quickly scan the story for key words and introduce these briefly before reading by pointing and labeling illustrations, for example.

When sharing stories or introducing new concepts, use props to help children understand the meaning of the words—for example, show them a stuffed zebra while introducing the English word *zebra*. Whenever possible, translate these key words into the children's home languages as well. Using children's home languages helps ensure that they will develop more balanced bilingual skills.

Give children **repeated opportunities to hear and use the new words** before, during, and after the story. Return to the same story several times over a week, or even longer, so children can practice using the words. Whenever possible, **read the book twice in a row**—once in English and once in the child's home language (if multiple languages are represented, group children by language). **Introduce book-related props throughout the room** to encourage discussions using the vocabulary and further support children's vocabulary development and comprehension.

Be aware of *how* language is used and the value attached to its use. For example, avoid the tendency to use a child's home language primarily to reprimand or set limits and English mainly during playtime or learning activities (Nemeth & Erdosi 2014). In addition, make efforts to facilitate communication between children who do not share the same language through intentionally planned experiences that reflect children's shared interests.

Physical Environment

For infants and toddlers who are learning two languages, organize the classroom environment so physical cues support their full participation in the program. For example, when creating labels, include pictures or photographs of the materials and words in each language represented in the room. Ask families and community members to assist with this effort. Use a different color for each language on the label—for example, always write the English word in blue, Spanish in red, Arabic in purple, and so on. (If needed for adults, add the phonetic pronunciation under the word.) These labels lay the groundwork for dual language print awareness and assure families of the program's commitment to linguistic inclusiveness. Over time, and with repeated exposure, young children learn that "their" languages are, for example, the blue and purple labels.

Pretend play props should include items used by children's families, such as slings (to carry dolls), a child-sized wok and chopsticks, a tortilla warmer, a mortar and pestle, and textiles (rugs, scarves, clothing) representing children's cultures. Involving families in this process is critical to ensure cultural sensitivity and appropriateness. Other props include empty food boxes contributed by families that include print in their home languages. In the book area, place books and community newspapers in families' home languages. Look for board books in children's home languages, especially less common languages, at local libraries or community organizations, or make them with the help of families and community members. Art, music, and other classroom materials (blankets, pillows, baskets, etc.) should reflect children's cultural backgrounds as well. These practices integrate young children's home cultures in tangible, age-appropriate ways.

When possible, keep the physical environment the same over time, resisting the impulse to rearrange furniture and materials regularly. Young children take cues from their environments, and in an unfamiliar language context, a stable physical setting can provide a sense of safety and security for dual language learners.

Supervision and Professional Development

Early educators need concrete strategies and skills for promoting children's development in both of their languages. Professional development can help teachers support children's continued home language development and deepen home–program connections as well.

A range of professional development strategies designed to support teachers' skills and children's dual language learning have been found to be effective in preschool settings. These include professional development institutes focused on supporting language and literacy development in dual language learners; individualized consultation from bilingual early childhood consultants to assist teachers in implementing key strategies for DLLs; and community of practice meetings (ongoing facilitated discussions among staff members to develop and refine instructional strategies for DLLs through shared inquiry and learning). Research on this combination of strategies found measurable improvements in teachers' language and literacy practices and strategies for dual language learners, and greater gains in children's home language phonological awareness skills (Buysse, Castro, & Peisner-Feinberg 2010). Infant/toddler programs can explore ways to adapt these professional development experiences in their settings.

During reflective supervision, a teacher and supervisor meet regularly to discuss the teacher's work with children and families and explore her perceptions of the issues and challenges that arise. This type of support is characterized by active listening and thoughtful, nonjudgmental questioning between a supervisor and teacher. Reflection empowers teachers to assess their own behaviors and make changes that are natural, unforced, and generated from within. Ongoing reflective supervision is helpful in the process of supporting very young dual language learners and their families because partnering with families whose beliefs and practices may be very different than one's own can be challenging and may elicit strong reactions in staff. Reflective supervision provides a safe environment for staff and supervisor to resolve these challenges in ways most likely to benefit the children, support the teacher's continued development, and strengthen relationships with families.

While all children benefit from high-quality early childhood settings, children at the beginning stages of learning English may *particularly* benefit (Goldenberg 2013) from such programs. High-quality teaching is typically characterized, in part, by highly trained early childhood staff, low child-to-staff ratios, and a language-rich environment. Program directors can work to ensure these elements are present in their infant/toddler programs.

Conclusion

Learning more than one language gives children a wide range of benefits—certainly linguistic and cognitive benefits, but social and emotional benefits as well. By retaining dual language skills throughout their lives, children can connect meaningfully with family and community members and develop a strong cultural identity. Programs for infants and toddlers can set the stage for this important growth and development. The path to truly inclusive environments for DLL infants and toddlers requires teachers to gain new understanding and make both major and minor adjustments in practice. Welcoming this change and embracing these differences is a mission of discovery—a journey along which infant/toddler professionals have many opportunities to make profound positive impacts on very young children and their families.

References

August, D., & T. Shanahan. 2006. *Developing Literacy in Second-Language Learners: Report of the National Literacy Panel on Language-Minority Children and Youth.* Mahwah, NJ: Lawrence Erlbaum.

Buysse, V., D.C. Castro, & E. Peisner-Feinberg. 2010. "Effects of a Professional Development Program on Classroom Practices and Outcomes for Latino Dual Language Learners." *Early Childhood Research Quarterly* 25 (2): 194–206.

Byers-Heinlein, K., T.C. Burns, & J.F. Werker. 2010. "The Roots of Bilingualism in Newborns." *Psychological Science* 21 (3): 343–48.

Castro, D.C., & L.M. Espinosa. 2014. "Developmental Characteristics of Young Dual Language Learners: Implications for Policy and Practice in Infant and Toddler Care." *Zero to Three* 34 (3): 34–40.

Castro, D.C., M.M. Páez, D.K. Dickinson, & E. Frede. 2011. "Promoting Language and Literacy in Young Dual Language Learners: Research, Practice, and Policy." *Child Development Perspectives,* 5 (1): 15–21.

Genesee, F. 2003. "Rethinking Bilingual Acquisition." In *Bilingualism: Challenges and Directions for Future Research,* ed. M. deWaele, 158–82. Clevedon, UK: Multilingual Matters.

Genesee, F., & E. Nicoladis. 2007. "Bilingual First Language Acquisition." In *Blackwell Handbook of Language Development,* eds. E. Hoff & M. Shatz, 324–42. Oxford, UK: Blackwell.

Gillanders, C., & D. Castro. 2007. "Reading Aloud to English Language Learners." *Children and Families* 21 (3): 12–14.

Goldenberg, C. 2013. "Unlocking the Research on English Learners: What We Know—and Don't Yet Know—About Effective Instruction." *American Educator* 37 (2): 4–11, 38. https://www.aft.org/pdfs/americaneducator/summer2013/Goldenberg.pdf.

Gutiérrez, K.D., M. Zepeda, & D.C. Castro. 2010. "Advancing Early Literacy Learning for All Children: Implications of the NELP Report for Dual-Language Learners." *Educational Researcher* 39 (4): 334–39.

Hart, B., & T.R. Risley. 1995. *Meaningful Differences in the Everyday Experiences of Young American Children.* Baltimore: Brookes.

Hoff, E., C. Core, S. Place, R. Rumiche, M. Señor, & M. Parra. 2012. "Dual Language Exposure and Early Bilingual Development." *Journal of Child Language* 39 (1), 1–27.

Klass, P. 2011, October 10. "Hearing Bilingual: How Babies Sort Out Language." The *New York Times.* www.nytimes.com/2011/10/11/health/views/11klass.html?_r=0.

Nemeth, K.N. 2012. *Many Languages, Building Connections: Supporting Infants and Toddlers Who Are Dual Language Learners.* Lewisville, NC: Gryphon House.

Nemeth, K.N., & V. Erdosi. 2014. "Enhancing Practice With Infants and Toddlers From Diverse Language and Cultural Backgrounds." In *Spotlight on Young Children: Supporting Dual Language Learners,* eds. M. Dombrink-Green & H. Bohart, 13–23. Washington, DC: NAEYC.

Parlakian, R., & S.Y. Sánchez. 2006. "Cultural Influences on Early Language and Literacy Teaching Practices." *The Journal of Zero to Three* 27 (1): 52–57.

Petitto, L.A., M. Katerelos, B.G. Levy, K. Gauna, K. Tétreault, & V. Ferraro. 2002. "Bilingual Signed and Spoken Language Acquisition From Birth: Implications for Mechanisms Underlying Bilingual Language Acquisition." *Journal of Child Language* 28 (2): 453–96.

Poulin-Dubois, D., A. Blaye, J. Coutya, & E. Bialystok. 2011. "The Effects of Bilingualism on Toddlers' Executive Functioning." *Journal of Experimental Child Psychology* 108 (3): 567–79.

U.S. Department of Health and Human Services, Office of Head Start. 2014. *Gathering and Using Information That Families Share.* Accessed August 5. www.eclkc.ohs.acf.hhs.gov/hslc/tta-system/cultural-linguistic/docs/dll_background_info.pdf.

Vihman, M.M., G. Thierry, J. Lum, T. Keren-Portnoy, & P. Martin. 2007. "Onset of Word Form Recognition in English, Welsh, and English-Welsh Bilingual Infants." *Applied Psycholinguistics* 28 (3): 475–93.

Karen N. Nemeth
and Valeria
Erdosi

Enhancing Practice With Infants and Toddlers From Diverse Language and Cultural Backgrounds

On Meili's first day at the center, her mother carries the 18-month-old into the classroom, whispering in Mandarin to the little girl. As she sets Meili down, the mom nervously smiles and nods to the teacher, then walks out the door. Not surprisingly, little Meili starts to cry. She runs after her mother, but the door has already closed. The adults try to comfort and distract Meili, but she doesn't understand a word they say. Meili has no idea when or if her mother will ever be back.

Many infants and toddlers whose families speak languages other than English have similar experiences when entering early childhood programs. While you think about Meili's stressful experience, imagine also what her mother must feel. She will be thinking of her daughter's desperate cries all day. When she returns to pick Meili up, the mother's lack of English skills will make it impossible for her to get information about how her daughter fared that first scary day. But what if this scenario were approached in a different way?

At The King's Daughters Day School, in Plainfield, New Jersey, Meili, a new-

Karen N. Nemeth, EdM, is the founder of Language Castle LLC, offering consultation and professional development on first and second language development. She is the author of *Basics of Supporting Dual Language Learners: An Introduction for Educators of Children From Birth Through Age 8* (NAEYC) and other resources for working with young children who are dual language learners.

Valeria Erdosi, MS, is the executive director of The King's Daughters Day School, in Plainfield, New Jersey. She is a founding member of the New Jersey Coalition of Infant/Toddler Educators and a well-known professional development provider.

Challenging Common Myths About DLLs

The language and literacy development of young DLLs follow pathways that are specific to children growing up with more than one language. DLLs may learn some shapes in their home language and some in English, and this knowledge is compartmentalized in the two languages separately until they get older. To fully understand what and how DLLs are learning and to support their successful learning of English, educators must observe what children know and can do in each language they use (p. 18).

comer to the infant/toddler room, was greeted with a few comforting words in Mandarin, even though the teachers speak mostly English. The teachers had asked Meili's parents about a few of her favorite songs so they could use them to help Meili feel more welcome and comfortable in her new surroundings. And when Meili's mother returned to pick up her daughter, a teacher showed her some digital photos of Meili happily playing during the day. A few simple steps can make all the difference in the experiences of children and families who bring different languages to infant and toddler care.

As infant/toddler programs encounter growing diversity, they need to reenvision the impact they have on children and families in all areas of practice, from recruiting new enrollees to stocking classrooms to changing the ways adults interact with children and families with different languages and from different cultures. What happens on the first day can set the stage for a family's involvement in a program.

The director and staff at The King's Daughters Day School, an NAEYC-Accredited early childhood program, take that responsibility very seriously. As one of the oldest child development programs in the United States (established in 1906), it holds a respected position in the small but diverse city of Plainfield. The day school serves children from infancy through school age, and there are 55 children in its five classrooms for infants and toddlers who can walk. At this writing, 60 percent of these children come from families with home languages other than English, including Spanish, Mandarin, Urdu, and indigenous South American dialects.

When an infant is separated from his parents and left in a new place, in the care of unfamiliar adults who speak a different language, all kinds of adjustments are necessary. A new language is only part of the picture. It is important to remember that "language is a cognitive process that is influenced by all domains of development, including motor, social, and emotional. Language acquisition is also influenced by the context in which the child grows, including family, the community, and the culture in which he or she lives" (Fort & Stechuk 2008, 24). Effective, developmentally appropriate strategies for supporting infants and toddlers who are dual language learners take into account all of these factors.

The home language is a child's connection to the love, nurturing, and lessons learned in the family context. Strengthening the bond between parent and child requires continual support of the home language. There are also cognitive advantages to building the home language while the child learns English. Research demonstrates that children who grow up bilingual have advanced self-regulation skills and advanced metalinguistic skills (Yoshida 2008). Growing up with two languages helps a child better understand how language works in general because she has to be more conscious of the features and rules of each of the languages. This understanding makes children more successful as language learners.

Parents and teachers need a common understanding and vision for rearing children with all the advantages of the families' rich cultural and linguistic heritages while also exposing the children to English (Notari-Syverson 2006). All early childhood professionals—teachers, home visitors, family child care monitors, college professors, program directors, trainers, nannies, consultants, therapists, early intervention providers, pediatricians, and social workers—need strategies to support the development of very young children and their families' cultural traditions in bilingual environments (Nemeth 2012).

All infants and toddlers need experiences that nurture, support, and teach their home language and culture, because this foundation is an important contributor to children's potential success in learning English. Even for infants, full immersion in an English-only program that reduces their experiences in their home language does not offer learning or developmental advantages (August & Shanahan 2006). Defining a commitment to addressing the language needs of each child in the program must be a team effort involving everyone who works or volunteers at the center, beginning with the leader or director. The developmentally appropriate strategies in this article address these key points.

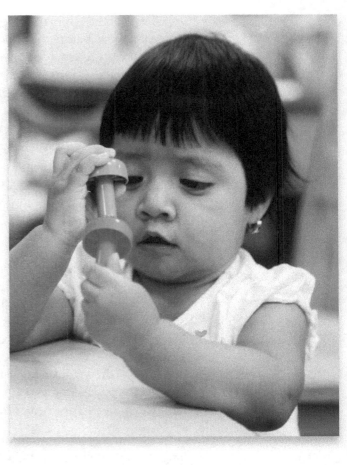

Building Connections With New Children and Families

The best way to build strong and mutually beneficial relationships with new and diverse families is to lay the foundation before those families enter the program. One way to get started is to build in time for parents to come to the program with their child for a few hours before leaving the child on a regular basis. The King's Daughters Day School asks parents to spend three mornings in the classroom with their child before the child officially starts. Here are other ways to connect with diverse families.

Reach out to diverse families in the community. Let families know that your program is prepared to welcome different languages and cultures. It sets the stage for a positive relationship with each potential client. The King's Daughters Day School prints flyers in English and Spanish and displays them at cultural festivals, public library branches, and other public locations.

Present a welcoming first impression that celebrates diversity. To help families feel they have chosen the right program, use pictures and languages on signs and displays that reflect the languages and cultures of the community. The King's Daughters Day School lines its driveway with small signs that say hello in different languages. Its entry hall displays photos of the diverse children who attend. Information for families is trimmed to as few words as possible, then translated into two or more languages, as the population requires.

Prepare before the child starts in your program. When you get to know each new family, be sure to learn exactly what language and dialect the family speaks at home. This will help you add appropriate classroom materials so the child sees himself reflected in the books, displays, and toys. Parents will also be more at ease if they see their language and some familiar images when they drop off their child on the first day. This can be a little difficult, but it evolves over time as families and staff build relationships.

> The best way to build strong and mutually beneficial relationships with new and diverse families is to begin to lay the foundation before those families enter the program.

A new child's primary caregiver should learn at least a few words in the family's home language before the child starts. Some programs send home a list of 10 to 15 key words and ask parents to make an audio recording in their home language or spell the words phonetically. If this does not work out, search online for translations. *Hello, up, down, change, diaper, clean, eat, juice, bottle, gentle, yes, no, more, hurt, mommy, daddy, outside, shoes, coat,* and *buckle* might be some words for your list. Knowing these words means that the teacher can say them to the child and recognize them if the child tries to communicate in his home language.

Help each family start in your program with confidence. Provide a list of items they should send in with their child—represent the items by photos to make sure the message is clear. Take the family on a tour of the center so the parents, other family members, and the child will feel at home.

Give a special welcome on the first day. It is most important to pause and focus on welcoming a new family with uncertain English skills, no matter how hectic sign-in time is. Say hello in the family's language, and be sure to pronounce the child's name correctly. Take a moment to hold the child and look at her. Does she have a runny nose you need to ask about? Does she appear sleepy or hungry? With a little extra effort and some nonverbal communication, a teacher can make important connections with the child and the parents. The teacher can demonstrate a successful drop-off experience—not too abrupt and not too drawn out. This is much easier to achieve if a parent or other family member has spent a few mornings in the program. A happy drop-off eliminates the infant's and family member's anxiety and the loneliness of not being able to communicate.

Equip the environment for diverse infants and toddlers. Representing each child's language and culture throughout the room is consistent with developmentally appropriate practice. This is important for children's self-esteem, and exposure to images from diverse cultures is valuable for all children. Visit the public library to find board books in the languages you need. Create posters using photos of the children's recognizable surroundings, such as their homes and families, the corner grocery, or the local park. Have

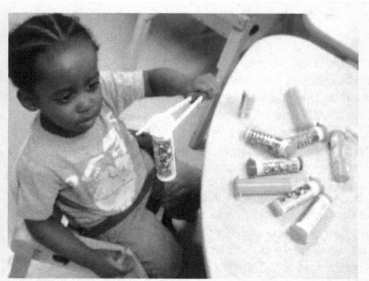

Practicing With Chopsticks

At The King's Daughters Day School, teachers plan a number of activities around the use of chopsticks. This is a wonderful example of helping all children become comfortable with a utensil that is commonplace in some cultures yet unheard of in others. All children benefit from practicing fine motor skills with chopsticks, pinching them to pick up small items and later using them to eat. Toddlers can easily use chopsticks if the sticks are attached at the top with small rubber bands. Other utensils from different cultures, such as a *tostonera* (a plantain press, for making *tostones*) from Cuba, help toddlers build skills and cultural awareness at the school.

diverse faces and skin colors in the doll area, the puzzle rack, and the small toy shelf. Represent familiar ethnic foods and cooking tools or other artifacts in the kitchen area. Labels in key areas of the room should have the words in the languages the children use as well as pictures. Even better, post phonetic spellings of key words in the different locations to remind teachers how to talk about play using the children's home languages.

Linguistically and Culturally Appropriate Practices

When teachers care for children who speak different languages they must think deeply and intentionally about how they use language with infants in general. Because the home language is so important to each child's family strengths, identity development, and language/literacy learning, teachers have to learn how to support both the home language and some English learning. Here are developmentally appropriate strategies to support all of these aspects of multilingual learning.

Foster a close teacher–child relationship. With different languages in an infant/toddler group, it is especially important that each child have a primary caregiver. Helping a child to navigate the learning of two or more languages requires the teacher to have a close relationship and a deep understanding of the infant or toddler. The teacher needs to be expert at reading the child's nonverbal signals, and the child has to be close enough to the teacher to understand the teacher's nonverbal signals as well.

Schedule home language and English use around routines. Be clear about separating the use of the two languages in a predictable way. Plan how and when you will use the child's home language and how and when you will use English each day. Some programs use English during play and use home languages during meals and snacks. Some programs use one language in the morning and the other in the afternoon. Even if a teacher is not fluent enough in the child's language to be able to devote half the day to its use, it is still important for him to learn key words—for example, the vocabulary needed to always use the home language at changing time and for morning greeting.

Stick with one language at a time. When you say a word in two languages, a child usually focuses on one language or the other. Instead, rely on tone of voice, body language, pictures, gestures, and props to make sure the child understands the words in the language you are using.

Staff at The King's Daughters Day School often use American Sign Language (ASL) as a gestural support to enhance spoken language. Teachers learn the signs from the many websites, books, and DVDs (available commercially and in libraries) that feature baby sign language. The advantage of using ASL signs is that one teacher's gesture for *eat* or *more* or *drink* is the same as the next teacher's, so the child can understand and use the same signs no matter where she is—in the program or beyond (Goodwyn, Acredolo, & Brown 2000). As a child tries to make sense of the words you are saying about changing his diaper, signing *change* helps him see the links between the English words and the home language words connected to the same activity.

Specialize in rich home language experiences. When a teacher is fluent in the home language of a child, he should plan times to use that language—and then use it with all the richness and interest that we know is critical to building early language and

With a little extra effort and some nonverbal communication, a teacher can make important connections with the child and the parents.

literacy. In some classrooms, bilingual staff use their other language only to manage the behavior of the young dual language learners, and all of the "teaching" occurs in English. Instead, staff should use their other languages in positive, engaging ways. Research shows that a strong foundation in the home language contributes to the successful acquisition of English (August & Shanahan 2006). The better support you provide for the home language, the more you are building a foundation for effective learning of English.

Be creative and imaginative. If a primary caregiver does not speak a child's home language, she can still support it by bringing in CDs (don't be afraid to ask parents) and singing songs in the language. Try using simple recorded stories or apps for smartphones or tablets that tell stories in different languages. It is essential to interact with the infant or toddler while listening to and watching media. Hold the child in your lap and repeat the interesting words and comment on the pictures. Welcome classroom volunteers—family members or community helpers—to spend time with the children. (If you do so, first give the volunteers a little training about how you expect them to interact with the infants and toddlers. See "Provide an Orientation for Classroom Volunteers.")

Based on the research of Patricia Kuhl (2010), we know that infants as young as 6 to 8 months can benefit from just a few hours a week of language support if it is delivered in person by a nurturing and familiar visitor. Kuhl's research shows that if that weekly language interaction is replaced by video or audio recordings of the same language, infants in that 6- to 8-month age range learn none of the language. With infants and toddlers, the only effective way to use televised or recorded language is for the adult to use it with the child or for the adult to use it for herself, as a tool to learn the words she can use with the child.

Support English. A solid foundation in language and preliteracy skills is critical for the development and school readiness of every child. What is important is that each young child grow, learn, and play every day in an environment filled with interesting words, one-on-one nurturing interactions, expression, wonder, discovery, and patience. In the first three years, it is possible that having this environment completely in a non-English language will help the later learning of English (August & Shanahan 2006). Having this environment almost entirely in English does not make English learning quicker or better in the long run (August & Shanahan 2006).

Exposing young dual language learners to English takes advantage of the brain's early language-learning openness. Still, remember that much of what a child knows has been stored in his brain in his home language. You may use a number of strategies to support his learning of English, but that doesn't mean he will know the same concepts in English if he first learned them in, say, a Spanish-speaking environment. For example, a child who has a pet cat at home will learn words and concepts about that cat—its care and habits—in her home language. If there are pet fish in the classroom, she may learn more about fish in English. The child might learn some related concepts, like eating and sleeping, in both languages, in both contexts. Other words and ideas may be picked up in one language but not yet transferred to the other language.

It is best not to turn language learning into a lesson. Just as we support a child's home language development by following her interests and engaging with her in exploring, repeating, and pretending, so we provide the same kinds of supports for the new language. Establishing communication skills is paramount in the first three years, as the child learns to get his needs met. Words add meaning to that communication as the child develops skills in one or more languages. Infant/toddler teachers need to share the experiences of the children in the here-and-now rather than preparing in advance activities or vocabulary lists.

Working Effectively With Diverse Families

Working with parents is one of the most important responsibilities of an infant/toddler teacher. When you and the parents speak a different language, it is harder to build an effective partnership. As populations change and diversity grows in all areas of the country, strategies for overcoming this obstacle are vital for everyone who works with infants and toddlers. Strategies that help you interact with non-English-speaking parents also help improve your communication with all families.

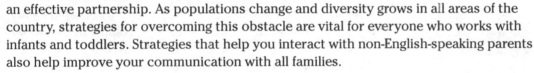

Offer activities to involve diverse parents—think outside the box. To accommodate families' various schedules, The King's Daughters Day School offers several options to participate in the program. Families may help plan the annual international festival, or they may bring some of their talents into the classroom, like writing Chinese characters for classroom labels.

Involving parents in the program offers multiple benefits: (a) parents see teachers model interactions and activities that can benefit their child; (b) teachers see parents and children interact and can offer support as needed; (c) teachers can learn to use some of the same strategies that a child's family uses for approaching, comforting, caregiving, and interacting; and (d) parents feel confident and connected to their child because they know and understand what the child does all day.

Some parents may prefer to help outside of the classroom—for example, making photocopies or cleaning toys or making furniture for the program. Offering options like these makes it more likely that you will find a way for every parent to get involved in the program and that you will get to know those parents.

Another tip for bringing parents into the program is to offer them something they feel they need, such as English as a second language classes, cultural cooking groups, or workshops on applying for jobs. These types of services can be more effective than offering parents something *you* think they need, such as a workshop on parenting. If you offer parent workshops and rarely get many parents to attend, it's time to broaden your thinking.

Create a family area. Create a welcoming area that encourages families to stop and sit a while, so they have time to talk to the teachers and each other. Some comfortable chairs, a pot of coffee and some cookies, and decorations related to the children's activities can create that kind of atmosphere. This may seem like a simple idea, but it actually is a very effective strategy in diverse programs because it encourages parents to slow down and get comfortable with the program, staff, and other families. Learning to communicate across language barriers takes a lot of time—time spent together—and plenty of opportunities to interact in pleasant, low-pressure situations to build the kind of rapport needed when you don't speak the same language as the family. When families rush in and out to drop off or pick up their children, or interact with staff only during stressful times such as reminders about overdue bills or parent–teacher conferences, they are less likely to overcome communication difficulties.

Support home literacy practices. This is one of infant/toddler teachers' most important strategies for involving parents in their children's learning! When programs do not have staff who speak the languages needed to read to all the children, it is particularly important to help families build home literacy practices. Establish a classroom lending library of age-appropriate books—wordless, bilingual, or written in the families' languages. Encourage families to bring in books in their home language to share. If the books are hard to find in the United States, families might obtain them during visits to or from relatives or on vacations. One source for books and materials in a variety of languages is www.languagelizard.com.

Demonstrate Interactive Reading

Reading to infants and toddlers may not come naturally to all parents. They may not see the point in reading to children who do not yet talk. They may lack confidence in their own reading abilities. Or they may not know or remember how much fun active, interactive reading can be. Programs need to show parents how to read with and tell stories to their young children. To make it easier for parents who don't speak your language, make a brief developmentally appropriate reading video to post on a site such as www.youtube.com or the program's website. Staff at The King's Daughters Day School provide a workshop to demonstrate to all parents how to read stories that capture their child's attention and build language skills.

Handling Difficult Conversations Across a Language Barrier

A number of challenging topics may come up in parent–teacher meetings, so it is best to establish a positive rapport with families before the need arises for a difficult conversation. Developing a trusting relationship across a language barrier takes a bit of extra effort. Sharing pictures and videos of their child's activities and accomplishments can help you and the parents begin to bond. The more time you spend together, the easier it will be to understand each other and to use nonverbal cues effectively.

Have an interpreter on hand. Ideally, when the time comes for an important conversation, a certified interpreter should be present. When this is not possible, ask a trusted staff member or a member of the family to help. Sometimes it is tempting to use another child in the family to interpret. Unless there is an emergency and no other choice, avoid this option, because this may place undue pressure on the other child, who may not have the maturity or fluency to interpret complex information. Programs need to find qualified staff who are bilingual, even if such teachers are not in every room where children speak their language. When staff at The King's Daughters Day School encounter an unfamiliar language, they seek help from community organizations and agencies, such as the local child care resource and referral agency or nearby communities of faith, to ensure that they are doing everything possible to communicate effectively with every parent. Remind conference participants about confidentiality.

Plan ahead. Prepare a message board with key phrases in English and in the family's home language, so that you and the child's family members can point to the information you want to communicate. Photographs of the child that show examples of the behavior or situation that led to the conversation may help parents understand what you are trying to say about their child. Google Translate is an online tool that lets you type your message and hear it spoken in another language. However, a computerized translation system may use words that are more applicable to businesses or tourism and not technically accurate for an early childhood discussion, so do not depend on it for everything. Ask the parents for permission to record your meeting so you can ask an interpreter to clarify what was said, even if the interpreter cannot be present during the initial meeting. This also allows you to make additional notes about the conversation and to notice any areas that did not seem clear and need to be addressed further.

Be aware of personal or cultural issues. Keep in mind that there may be personal and/or cultural differences with regard to holding a parent–teacher meeting. Some cultures give less attention to on-time arrivals than others. Some parents may bring their whole family to a meeting with the teacher, and others may be so embarrassed that they won't even tell their family about the meeting. Do not assume that the parents will be comforted by a hug or by taking their hand. It is usually best to ask first.

Keep the message clear and brief. One of the hardest yet most effective strategies for holding conferences with parents who speak other languages is to say a lot less than you usually do. Prepare in advance by carefully reducing your messages to only the most critical and factual information. This makes it easier for translation and interpretation and more likely that the parents will come away with some real understanding. If you need to ask the family to do something, such as pick up their child earlier or take the child to the doctor or seek an evaluation, try to state that goal as simply and clearly as possible, then stick to a very few clear observations to explain your concerns.

Allow time to digest the information. Difficult messages are never easy to hear. They can be even more challenging for people who are not sure they understand everything you say and are not sure how to ask important questions. For these reasons, it may be

> **Engaging Families**
>
> Some parents worry that their children will not learn English if they continue to hear their home language spoken in the early childhood setting. For example, Salma, a native Urdu speaker and mother of 2-year-old Farida, was concerned when she arrived at the center to pick up her daughter one day. Farida and another child were playing with their teacher, Carmen, who was chatting with them in Urdu. The children were pointing to objects and saying the Urdu words for them.
>
> Salma wondered why Carmen was speaking to Farida in Urdu, as she felt Farida needed to learn English. Carmen explained that very young children can and do learn two or more languages at the same time. The program supported bilingualism to validate children's home languages, develop their sense of self, and help children maintain connections to their extended families and cultures. She told Salma that the children *were* learning English, as this was the language the teachers used during group times and also during routines like snack time. They spoke Urdu during playtime. Carmen reassured Salma that, for young children, learning two languages does not come at the expense of either language.

Establish a classroom lending library of age-appropriate books—wordless, bilingual, or written in the families' languages.

best to plan the conversation over two meetings, allowing time for the family to absorb and think about the information. Then the parties can get back together to plan ways to resolve the issue. Keep in mind that a parent–teacher conference is a two-way conversation, not a lecture. Leave enough time for the parents to ask questions before agreeing on next steps.

Resolve differences that are based on language or cultural issues. As well as being culture based, some child-rearing differences "may result from a family tradition, an individual experience, specific kinds of training, and philosophical ideals" (Gonzalez-Mena 2009). It is not essential that you know every cultural belief and practice for each group represented in your care. Rather, it is important that you get to know each family and what is important to them.

A family enrolls their 2-year-old in an early childhood program. The director places him in the older toddler classroom, where he seems to adjust well. The mother spends several hours in the room with him on the first day. On the second day, and for a number of days thereafter, the mother leaves the child but returns at lunchtime to spoon-feed him his entire meal.

The teacher has a strong negative reaction to the child's being fed. She feels it is critical for a 2-year-old to practice self-help skills, and she voices her reservations to the parents. The parents stand their ground, explaining that in their culture, feeding a young child is a sign of love and caring.

Over time, the teacher and parents learn to listen to each other. Everyone takes a step back and arrives at a compromise: the parents will gradually reduce the number of days a week they arrange to feed their son, and the teacher will help the family find activities that the child can use to develop self-help skills in other ways.

Conclusion

Sharing pictures and videos of their child's activities and accomplishments can help you and the parents begin to bond.

It may take practice to become comfortable with varied cultural and familial practices—especially the ones that seem counterproductive to you. A strong sense of self-awareness will help you detect whether you are really looking out for a child's best interests or whether you are just trying to make the family do things your way. Mutual respect between you and the children's families will help you know and understand them as individuals and as family units, including all the unique characteristics and cultural practices that make them who they are. Knowing the child, his interests, his family context, his culture, and his language is important in implementing developmentally appropriate practice.

Fort and Stechuk remind us that young children need support for their home language for social-emotional reasons as well as for cognitive reasons: "In a place where no one speaks the child's language and knows very little of his culture, a child could feel lost, misunderstood, and alienated" (2008, 24). Early care and education professionals can use developmentally appropriate practices that encompass a child's social and emotional needs in the context of facilitating the development of both English and the home language. According to Rebecca Parlakian, "Social-emotional skills are an integral part of school readiness because they give very young children the skills they need to communicate, cooperate, and cope in new environments" (2004, 39). Infant/toddler teachers can develop skills, learn strategies, and find resources that greatly enhance their success with diverse children and families. It may take extra work, but the benefits can last a lifetime.

References

August, D., & T. Shanahan, eds. 2006. *National Literacy in Second-Language Learners: Report of the National Literacy Panel on Language—Minority Children and Youth*. Mahwah, NJ: Erlbaum.

Fort, P., & R. Stechuk. 2008. "The Cultural Responsiveness and Dual Language Education Project." *Zero to Three* 29 (1): 24–28.

Freedman, S.E., & J.A. Barlow. 2012. "Using Whole-Word Production Measures to Determine the Influence of Phonotactic Probability and Neighborhood Density on Bilingual Speech Production." *International Journal of Bilingualism* 16 (4): 369–87.

Gonzalez-Mena, J. 2009. *Fifty Strategies for Communicating and Working With Diverse Families*. 2nd ed. Boston: Pearson.

Goodwyn, S.W., L.P. Acredolo, & C. Brown. 2000. "Impact of Symbolic Gesturing on Early Language Development." *Journal of Nonverbal Behavior* 24 (2): 81–103.

Ithaca College. 2013. "Bilingual Children Have a Two-Tracked Mind." ScienceDaily. www.sciencedaily.com/releases/2013/07/130715151106.htm.

Kuhl, P. "The Linguistic Genius of Babies." Filmed October 2010. TED video, 10:18. Posted February 2011. www.ted.com/talks/patricia_kuhl_the_linguistic_genius_of_babies.html.

Nemeth, K.N. 2012. *Many Languages, Building Connections: Supporting Infants and Toddlers Who Are Dual Language Learners*. Lewisville, NC: Gryphon House.

Notari-Syverson, A. 2006. "Everyday Tools of Literacy." Chap. 3 in *Learning to Read the World: Language and Literacy in the First Three Years*, eds. S.E. Rosenkoetter & J. Knapp-Philo, 61–80. Washington, DC: ZERO TO THREE.

Parlakian, R. 2004. "Early Literacy and Very Young Children." *Zero to Three* 25 (1): 37–44.

Rosenkoetter, S.E., & J. Knapp-Philo, eds. 2006. *Learning to Read the World: Language and Literacy in the First Three Years*. Washington, DC: ZERO TO THREE.

Yoshida, H. 2008. "The Cognitive Consequences of Early Bilingualism." *Zero to Three* 29 (2): 26–30.

Elizabeth S. Magruder, Whitcomb W. Hayslip, Linda M. Espinosa, and Carola Matera

Many Languages, One Teacher:
Supporting Language and Literacy Development for Dual Language Learners

naeyc® 2, 3

In a classroom of 4-year-olds three children are actively engaged during center-based learning. One small group constructs a tower using blocks of all sizes. This is a specific structure the group decided to make after listening to a nonfiction book—*Structures*, by Time-Life Books—about all sizes and types of structures. As the group builds, Mrs. Blakley observes the interactions and listens to the following dialogue:

José: We make a scraper.

Thomas: Like a skyscraper! We have to make it tall. Keep putting more blocks.

José: Yeah, make it tall—like a scraper. *(The three children each add blocks to the tower until it almost reaches their shoulders, and it begins to fall over.)*

Cindy: Oh, no! Too high! Too high!

Thomas: We have to put blocks down here to make it strong.

Cindy: Let's make it strong! Strong tower!

José: Strong scraper!

Thomas: If we don't make it strong, the skyscraper will fall!

José, Cindy, and Thomas are all at different stages of language development. José is a dual language learner (DLL) in the early stages of English language acquisition; Cindy is a DLL who speaks both Spanish and English at home; and Thomas is a native English speaker. From this interaction, Mrs. Blakley (a fictitious teacher, based on the authors' observations of numerous practitioners in the field) learns that this small group activity provides the time, space, and materials for the children to understand and practice key vocabulary through engaging and meaningful play. This observation will guide her future decisions about targeted instruction for language development. It also sparks some essential questions about José in particular:

♦ What home language skills does José bring with him?

♦ What kinds of language-learning exposure and opportunities does José experience at home?

♦ How can José's knowledge in his home language be activated and applied to the task of learning English?

♦ How can Mrs. Blakley, a monolingual English speaker, promote José's growth in both English language development and home language skills?

Mrs. Blakley's classroom is culturally and linguistically diverse, representing more than five different languages and ethnicities. While some of the children have been identified as DLLs, Mrs. Blakley has determined through ongoing observation and child assessments that most of the children will need focused support in language development. She needs to intentionally design lessons, activities, and interactions that capitalize on the linguistic knowledge the children bring with them while she systematically fosters English language development.

Challenging Common Myths About DLLs

Young DLLs benefit socially and cognitively from their emerging bilingualism if they receive consistent, meaningful support of their home language while they are also learning English. This support can be provided even if teachers do not speak children's home languages by stocking classrooms with books, music, and materials in the children's languages and by engaging staff, volunteers, and family members in the child's learning activities (p. 11).

Dual Language Learning

The US Census Bureau projects that by the 2030s, children whose home language is other than English will increase from roughly 22 percent to 40 percent of the school-age population. The numbers are growing even more rapidly for the preschool years due to increasing immigration and birth rates (Center for Public Education 2012). The diversity of languages and ethnicities among children entering early education programs is growing as well, with, for example, more than 43 percent of California's public school enrollment comprised of children who speak a language other than English in their homes (California Department of Education 2014).

Because DLLs represent a growing proportion of pre-K–12 children, and their educational achievement has consistently lagged behind their native English-speaking peers, improving the conditions of DLLs' early schooling and their long-term educational attainment is an urgent concern to educators at all levels (Espinosa 2010). Research indicates that becoming proficient in two languages is both possible for and beneficial to young children; bilingual preschoolers show cognitive, linguistic, and social-emotional advantages (Bialystok 2008; Kuhl 2009). Two research synthesis reports, published in 2006 by the National Literacy Panel and the Center for Research on Education, Diversity, and Excellence, find that DLLs benefit from instruction that focuses on decoding and comprehension in English. The reports also conclude that a strong home-language base makes it easier to learn English, and that young children can learn two languages as naturally as learning one (August & Shanahan 2006; Genesee 2010; Castro, Ayankoya, & Kasprzak 2011).

Unless teachers and families make an effort to support both the home language and English, young DLLs can easily lose the ability to speak and understand their home language, or lose the balance between the two languages (Puig 2010; Castro, Ayankoya, & Kasprzak 2011). If young children lose the language of their home, they will never experience the many advantages of becoming fully bilingual. They might find communicating with elder family members difficult and feel less connected to their family traditions and heritage. This disconnect can lead to emotional and self-esteem concerns as DLLs approach adolescence (Wong Fillmore 1991).

For all these reasons, supporting and encouraging young children's dual language learning makes sense and is crucial to their long-term success.

Language and Communication

When children have a safe, nurturing, and culturally and linguistically responsive environment in which to learn, they communicate their experiences and discoveries in a multitude of ways.

The more interesting and interactive the conversations are that children take part in, the more language they learn. Reading books, singing, playing word games, and simply talking to and with children builds their vocabulary while providing increased opportunities to develop listening skills. Children learn by engaging in daily interactions and experiences with peers and skilled adults. Between the ages of 4 and 5, many children enter preschool programs, making language competency vital for navigating and participating in the classroom community. DLLs come to early childhood programs with richly varied backgrounds, sets of skills, and cultural ways of knowing: they need teachers who welcome them and recognize their unique abilities, what they know, and what they need to learn. Teachers of young DLLs understand that children communicate their knowledge using the safest method possible, and this may mean the use of their home language, English, or a mixture of both.

Mrs. Blakley elicits the help of community volunteers to support dual language learners. Her classroom reflects the children's languages and cultures with greetings, alphabets, and key phrases written in each child's home language. The environmental print reflects child-created labels; a library corner features literature in various home languages; and cozy learning spaces allow children to interact around interesting and familiar topics.

Personalized Oral Language(s) Learning

Early childhood educators understand that oral language development is a critical component of later reading success. While teachers employ numerous strategies and approaches to support oral language development, it can be challenging to provide targeted attention to each child. Curriculum and lesson planning provide guidance on the *what* and the *when* of teaching, but rarely on the *how*. How can we, as teachers, personalize oral language experiences for children, especially DLLs? How can we expand and

Elizabeth S. Magruder, MEd, is an educational consultant supporting early childhood education programs throughout California. Elizabeth has worked on multiple projects that focus on dual language learners, stemming from her 22 years of teaching and coaching experience.

Whitcomb W. Hayslip, MA, is an independent consultant supporting a number of early childhood education projects throughout California. He previously served as the assistant superintendent, early childhood education, for the Los Angeles Unified School District.

Linda M. Espinosa, PhD, is the coprincipal investigator for the Center for Early Care and Education Research–Dual Language Learners at Frank Porter Graham CDI at the University of North Carolina, Chapel Hill, and lead consultant for the Best Practices for Young Dual Language Learners Project at the California State Department of Education, Child Development Division.

Carola Matera, PhD, is an assistant professor of early childhood studies at California State University Channel Islands. Carola has worked on topics related to teaching and supporting young dual language learners' learning and development.

enrich what we teach and, at the same time, give children multiple opportunities throughout the day to practice? What strategies can we use consistently, as part of the daily routine, to broaden and enhance oral language development? What should these enhancements be and how can we integrate them into lesson plans and long-range goals?

While working with groups of teachers supporting dual language learners in California, the authors recognized the critical need to both provide more intensive and individualized support in oral language development to all children and explicitly help DLLs apply what they already know about language to the task of learning English. To meet this need, three of the authors, in collaboration with Whitcomb Hayslip, the district administrator at the time, designed Personalized Oral Language(s) Learning (POLL) for the Los Angeles Unified School District. This program gives teachers a specific set of strategies and practices to increase the effectiveness of language and literacy instruction for all young children, but with a focus on young DLLs. The developers derived the POLL features by evaluating current research on best practices for literacy instruction in general, and then designing a fine-tuned approach that focuses on oral language learning in young children, especially dual language learners.

Components of POLL

1. Families First

When teachers and families connect early on *and* in person, they establish a common goal to support the child both at home and in school. Families and teachers together are champions for the child and share responsibility in supporting language and learning goals.

Family languages and interests interview. The purpose of this interview is for families to tell teachers about their children's home language practices, talents, and interests, to better connect family, teacher, and child, and to promote home–school connections. Conduct the interview in person during the first weeks of school as a way to welcome families, establish a rapport, and discuss some shared language and learning goals. The information gathered provides the framework for inviting families into the preschool setting, as well as preparing environmental and teaching supports early on, such as displaying relevant cultural artifacts and providing books and materials written in children's home languages.

Engaging Families

Ms. Barbara had been observing Alma, a new child in the preschool program, for a few weeks. Ms. Barbara had noticed that Alma rarely spoke in class, but she seemed to understand directions and happily engaged in activities, following the other children's lead. One day Alma was block building with Lisa. Lisa held on to the base and excitedly told Alma, "Put on more!" Alma smiled at Lisa and added more blocks.

One afternoon Alma's mother and grandmother picked her up from preschool. Ms. Barbara invited them in and encouraged Alma to give them a tour of the classroom. As Alma showed them around, Barbara noticed that Alma spoke to them in Russian. During Ms. Barbara's initial meeting with Alma's parents they had indicated that they spoke English at home. Before they left, Ms. Barbara talked more with Alma's mother and grandmother and learned that Alma's grandma was her primary caregiver. This discussion helped Ms. Barbara realized that Alma was a dual language learner and in the early stages of English acquisition. It also reinforced for Ms. Barbara the importance of gathering complete family background information. Ms. Barbara's new insight into Alma's home language, along with daily observations, helped her make adjustments to appropriately support Alma's language development in both Russian and English.

2. Environmental Supports

The classroom's physical environment sets the stage for active and engaged learning. It conveys a crucial message to children that they will be safe, nurtured, and valued. It is important for the design and layout of the classroom to offer established learning spaces that engage children's interest and promote conversations in both large and small groups.

The physical environment is nurturing and engaging. Look at the environment through the eyes of the child. Think about colors, learning spaces, supplies, furniture, accessibility, warmth. Is it child centered, cocreated, inviting, user friendly, interesting, and safe? Can children *actively* participate in all learning areas? For example, can the classroom rug (where children gather for whole group experience) later be used for play-based learning with building blocks?

Learning centers support and promote conversations around exploration and discovery and are linked to study themes. Intentionally plan and prepare centers to achieve targeted language and learning goals. These areas evolve as children evolve. Teachers are observers and facilitators while children interact. Use center time as an opportunity to both engage with children and provide language support in the moment, while listening to and observing what children say and do.

Print-rich labeling is visible and represents all home languages. Label areas and supplies in English and children's home languages. Include a photograph of the item on each label to visually support the languages that are written. For monolingual English-speaking teachers, learning words and phrases in home languages fosters a collaborative and culturally responsive classroom community in which all children are valued. When learning key words in home languages, invite children to cocreate and help write the labels!

Books, materials, displays, and artifacts reflect all languages, cultures, families, and communities of children. Showcase books (library corner), artifacts, and materials (featured exhibit/discovery table) in areas where children can gather to explore. Encourage children and families to bring in relevant artifacts and materials to share.

3. Instructional Supports

Integrate POLL strategies throughout the day and provide extended activities across contexts to reinforce children's learning of new concepts and vocabulary, placing the emphasis on children's experiences.

Intentional message: A written message, with embedded content vocabulary, that sets the purpose of each lesson and is displayed where children can see it and refer to it.

The message can be prewritten or cowritten with the children, depending on the instructional purpose, such as a shared writing or interactive writing session. Think about preteaching (teaching concepts in advance) the words in home languages to support concept development (e.g., *amigos* [friends], *cantar* [to sing]).

Example: During circle time: "Welcome, **friends!** I am happy to see you. I like to **sing.** What do you like to do?"

During math time: "Today we will be **mathematicians** and **explore** which **group** of blocks has **more.**"

What Mrs. Blakley learned: "The intentional message provides a framework for the content and lesson I am about to teach. It gives the children a goal that the whole class will work on during that day. They know what to expect, and it's another way for them to process the vocabulary words that are central to understanding that day's lessons."

Anchor text: An intentionally selected picture book used repeatedly to foster vocabulary and concept development.

Teachers can use an anchor text in multiple ways and for many purposes with dual language learners. The following suggestions are ways to support DLLs' language and literacy development using the anchor text as a tool.

- ◆ Choose three to five key vocabulary words from a picture book to introduce throughout the week. Learn these key words in children's home languages before reading the book in class, then preteach the text and vocabulary to dual language learners (in home languages and English) in small groups before introducing it to the whole class.

- ◆ Implement reading strategies with DLLs (e.g., *dialogic reading*—a read-aloud that includes brief interactions between the teacher and the children), one-on-one or in small groups (no more than two), to prepare for whole group reading.

- ◆ Seek support from parents or community volunteers to assist the children in the classroom with home language needs.

- ◆ Remember that picture books can be adapted and read in any language! Seek out parents or community members who can help.

Example: Before introducing an anchor text to the whole class, one or two days in advance ask a small group of dual language learners to teach you key words in their language. This bridges concepts and language learning while providing context and meaning for the upcoming lesson.

What Mrs. Blakley learned: "I usually have three or four key books in mind when I teach a particular unit or concept. My directed lessons took place during and after reading the book with the whole class. I often supported dual language learners in the moment or after whole group and rarely used *home language bridging,* in which a recognized concept in the home language is transferred to English. I learned that in planning and preparing ahead of time, DLLs can actively participate in whole group activities with more confidence, having spent concentrated time with me or a community volunteer beforehand. This is so important for their self-esteem and for their language acquisition."

Vocabulary imprinting: The use of photographs, images, and word walls to introduce new concepts and vocabulary and deepen comprehension.

Example: Use photographs with labels, recipes, magazine cutouts, children's photos or drawings from home, vocabulary walls, and cognate walls (displaying words in two languages that share a similar meaning, spelling, and pronunciation).

What Mrs. Blakley learned: "I used to post vocabulary words on the wall with a picture next to it for display, and the children and I would refer to it often. Now I make it more interactive. I learn key words ahead of time in the children's home languages and make a list of cognates. In our lessons, we cocreate a list of cognates and benefit from seeing patterns and connecting words in multiple languages. I now have key words and photos in a pocket chart so children can come up at any time during the day, pull them out, and work with them interactively."

Visual cues/gestures: Physical movements, repeated to imprint meaning as specific content vocabulary is introduced.

Example: Choose movements/gestures for a few key words only, and repeatedly use these gestures throughout the day and week so that children begin to link the gestures with words and concepts. For example, with the key word *explore,* the gesture could be to extend a flat hand up to your eyebrows and look back and forth.

What Mrs. Blakley learned: "Using gestures and movements for key words really makes learning fun! All children can participate. I went a bit overboard at first with pairing gestures to many words and found that it was too much for us to remember. Choosing a few movements for the more difficult words was more effective. We used the gestures more frequently and it helped the children learn and understand meaning in a deeper way."

Songs/chants: Content vocabulary woven into familiar songs and chants to encourage repetition.

Example: The "More" chant.
Key vocabulary: More, greater, bigger, few, less.

More means *greater* and *greater means more.*
More is *bigger* than ever before!
More is *many* while *few* is *less.*

My songs and chants tend to rhyme because this age group responds so enthusiastically to those sound patterns.

More is a lot—no need to guess!
More means *greater* and *greater* means *more.*
More is *bigger* than ever before!

What Mrs. Blakley learned: "Children love music and movement. I use the chants all day long and for many different purposes. What I didn't realize at first is that I could teach strategic vocabulary with them. When I create chants and songs using key words that we are working on, it is another way the children can learn new words. My songs and chants tend to rhyme because this age group responds so enthusiastically to those sound patterns."

Center extensions: Planned center-based opportunities for independent and/or small group practice. These are child directed and teacher facilitated.

Example: After teaching a math lesson using bear counters and work mats, place these materials in the math center to allow children time and space to explore concepts on their own and collaboratively. This encourages practice and repetition and fosters problem solving, interaction, and rich discussion.

What Mrs. Blakley learned: "I look at center time as an opportunity for the children to interact with each other and talk, talk, talk! I observe and facilitate conversations around learning and, most important, I listen! The dual language learners get so much out of this time. They have the opportunity to work with same-language friends and English-speaking models. It is a much more enriching experience now."

Conclusion

By integrating the foundational elements of POLL in her daily planning, Mrs. Blakley deepens her teaching practices and strengthens her connection with families. The focus on personalizing oral language interactions provides all the children with more language learning opportunities and supports the dual language learners with a deeper and more connected approach. She says, "I am able to observe and make intentional modifications for José and Cindy. With POLL planning, I know what my next steps will be for them."

Mrs. Blakley has found ways to elicit support for DLLs from community volunteers and parents who assist from home and in the classroom: "I now have additional tools and a more thoughtful approach to strengthen and support the children's language needs, which make teaching vocabulary and comprehension so meaningful and fun! Children feel appreciated, safe, valued. I feel good knowing I have ways to better support multiple languages in the classroom, even though I speak only English."

Intentionality in goal setting, planning, instruction, and observation is critical. The commitment of teachers to plan strategically for all children, especially dual language learners, requires thoughtful planning and continuous preparation. The enhanced personal connections and increased language learning opportunities that occur with POLL help the classroom come alive for both children and teachers.

References

August, D., & T. Shanahan, eds. 2006. *Developing Literacy in Second-Language Learners: Report of the National Literacy Panel on Language-Minority Children and Youth.* Mahwah, NJ: Erlbaum.

Bialystok, E. 2008. "Cognitive Effects of Bilingualism Across the Lifespan." In *BUCLD 32: Proceedings of the 32nd Annual Boston University Conference on Language Development,* eds. H. Chan, H. Jacob, & E. Kapia, 1–15. Boston: Cascadilla Press.

California Department of Education. 2014. "Facts About English Learners in California." *CalEdFacts.* Sacramento: California Department of Education. Accessed September 16. www.cde.ca.gov/re/pn/fb/index.asp.

Castro, D.C., B. Ayankoya, & C. Kasprzak. 2011. *The New Voices, Nuevas Voces Guide to Cultural and Linguistic Diversity in Early Childhood.* Baltimore: Brookes.

Center for Public Education. 2012. "The United States of Education: The Changing Demographics of the United States and Their Schools." www.centerforpubliceducation.org/You-May-Also-Be-Interested-In-landing-page-level/Organizing-a-School-YMABI/The-United-States-of-education-The-changing-demographics-of-the-United-States-and-their-schools.html.

Espinosa, L.M. 2010. "Assessment of Young English Language Learners." Chap. 7 in *Young English Language Learners: Current Research and Emerging Directions for Practice and Policy,* eds. E.E. García & E.C. Frede, 119–42. New York: Teachers College Press.

Genesee, F. 2010. "Dual Language Development in Preschool Children." Chap. 4 in *Young English Language Learners: Current Research and Emerging Directions for Practice and Policy,* eds. E.E. García & E.C. Frede, 59–79. New York: Teachers College Press.

Kuhl, P.K. 2009. "Early Language Acquisition: Neural Substrates and Theoretical Models." Chap. 57 in *The Cognitive Neurosciences,* 4th ed., ed. M.S. Gazzaniga, 837–54. Cambridge, MA: MIT Press.

Puig, V.I. 2010. "Are Early Intervention Services Placing Home Languages and Cultures 'At Risk'?" *Early Childhood Research and Practice* 12 (1). http://ecrp.uiuc.edu/v12n1/puig.html.

Wong Fillmore, L. 1991. "Second-Language Learning in Children: A Model of Language Learning in Social Context." Chap. 3 in *Language Processing in Bilingual Children,* ed. E. Bialystok, 49–69. Cambridge, UK: Cambridge University Press.

Joan Youngquist and Bárbara Martínez-Griego

Learning in English, Learning in Spanish:
A Head Start Program Changes Its Approach

kagit/Islands Head Start (SIHS) in Washington State has always taken pride in its high-quality learning program. But we discovered a problem: the child assessments from 13 centers serving children from birth to age 5 indicated that although Spanish-speaking 3-year-olds entered with language and literacy skills at a level similar to their English-speaking peers, a year later they were lagging behind in their Spanish language skills.

As the director of Skagit Islands Head Start (Joan) and the early childhood program manager (Bárbara), this finding concerned us greatly. Approximately 60 percent of enrolled families were Latino, with 40 percent speaking Spanish as their home language. We knew

that the Latino children's learning success was at risk because statistics from our local high school showed that 50 percent of Latino boys dropped out of school. We also knew that the stage for school failure is set early.

What surprised us was seeing an early discrepancy in our own program! Our staff recognized the value of a child's home language and regularly translated information for families into Spanish. In addition, whenever possible, we hired classroom staff who spoke at least some Spanish. However, upon close inspection, we discovered that our classrooms were inconsistent and inadequate in supporting children's home languages. While our local

naeyc® 2, 3, 10

Joan Youngquist, PhD, is dean of Basic Education and Academic Transfer programs and executive director of Skagit/Islands Head Start at Skagit Valley College in Mount Vernon, Washington. She has more than 20 years of experience as a teacher and an administrator in multicultural early learning programs.

Bárbara Martínez-Griego, MA, is chair of the Early Childhood Education Department and lead instructor at Skagit Valley College. She teaches child development courses in Spanish and English, infusing them with strategies for working effectively with bilingual children and families. Bárbara is a co-researcher in the Teaching Umoja Participatory Action Research project in Kingston, Jamaica. She has worked as an elementary school teacher, preschool teacher, Head Start program administrator, and child care licensor.

program guidance emphasized English immersion, staff differed in their beliefs and approaches. Some held to the English immersion model; others tried their best to teach in two languages. Many non-English-speaking families wanted their children to learn English quickly, and some stopped speaking Spanish at home and tried speaking what English they could to their children. This created a situation in which children failed to receive a solid foundation in any language during a crucial time in their language development.

Aware of all these factors, we knew it was time to reevaluate our local program guidance, which was based on two assumptions: all children need to be fluent in English by kindergarten and the best way to accomplish this is through a total English immersion approach in the classroom. These assumptions were due to common practice, limited knowledge, and a lack of expertise available in the community. To change our practices that we based on these assumptions would be difficult, we knew. And to be successful, change must be thoughtful, intentional, and take place over time. To begin, we initiated an intentional multistep, multiyear process to transform the approach to language and learning in our classrooms.

Step 1

Refining the Vision and Defining a Paradigm Shift

The SIHS vision was and *is* that all children succeed in learning now and when they continue on to kindergarten and the higher grades. The program's dual language learners (DLLs) were not achieving this goal. Thus, the first step in changing our language-learning approach was for both staff and families to understand the important role language plays in achieving this vision. Support of program directors and management staff was essential, and one of us (Bárbara) took the lead in researching language learning and presenting our findings to the management staff.

Research supports the need for children to develop a strong foundation and learn concepts in their home language, and it identifies the cognitive benefit in learning two languages as long as children have a strong foundation, primarily oral language and listening, in their home language (Bialystok 2001; Cronin, Lenear, & Sosa Massó 2013).We learned that when young children are learning more than one language, both languages follow the typical development process, and this does not cause language disorders or substantive language delays (Lee 1996; Cronin, Lenear, & Sosa Massó 2013). Children may sometimes mix both languages within sentences (for example, "*vamos* outside"), but this tendency resolves itself as language proficiencies increase (Quiñones-Eatman 2001).

Research consistently points to significant social, emotional, cultural, economic, and linguistic gains when children become bilingual early in life:

◆ DLLs with a strong foundation in their home language learn to read, write, and speak in English faster than children who do not have that foundation (Cummins 1992).

◆ Preventing children from developing their home language can have a negative impact on academic achievement (Sanchez & Thorp 1998).

- Young children can become increasingly fluent in a second language if they have opportunities to speak it with a variety of individuals, on a variety of topics, and for a variety of reasons (Quiñones-Eatman 2001).

- Failure to learn the primary home language well can be a source of identity confusion for children and be harmful to family function (Makin, Jones Díaz, & McLachlan 2007).

- Children in bilingual school programs outperform comparable monolingual students in academic

subjects after four to six years of dual language education. A bilingual program must meet a child's developmental needs, including the academic, cognitive, emotional, social, and physical. Schools should create a learning environment with lots of natural and rich oral and written experiences in each language instead of providing translations (Thomas & Collier 2002).

With this knowledge to guide our planning, we began a very intentional process of changing the program paradigm from "English immersion is the road to success" to "A strong foundation in a home language is essential for success."

Step 2
Raising Staff Awareness

To *describe* a paradigm shift is one thing, but it is quite another for management to make it happen in a large, geographically and culturally diverse organization. SIHS enrolls 97 children in Early Head Start and 348 preschoolers in 13 centers in Skagit Island and San Juan counties of western Washington. Demanding that staff change their practices would obviously only create resentment, so we began by having lots of conversations. Management staff shared questions with each other during weekly staff meetings, with classroom staff, and with coauthor Bárbara, who offered her knowledge and research findings indicating what was best for children.

Questions and doubts raised by teachers caused us to look even deeper into research and to develop more knowledge on the topic. Bárbara wrote articles in the staff newsletter based on her experience, the research, and her observations of children in our program. The management team established a new program committee—the Multicultural Committee—to explore the question of home language learning and the broader issue of cultural awareness in which the issue rested. This talk continued for about a year, and some frustration set in among the staff and Bárbara. Bárbara felt that her knowledge and expertise were not convincing enough for staff and that, as is often true for an organization, an outside expert could be more effective in demonstrating that change was necessary and possible.

Step 3

Solidifying Staff by Bringing in Outside Expertise

Our location near Seattle, a large metropolitan center, had advantages, such as access to Pacific Oaks College. Faculty member Sharon Cronin was well known for her work and expertise in the area of supporting home language and culture. Bárbara invited her to present a one-day training for all SIHS staff. Through lecture, group activities, music, and games, Cronin effectively communicated the importance of supporting learning in a child's home language.

Literacy is more than reading books and counting and reciting the alphabet, staff learned as they began to see the importance of communicating with children in a variety of ways—through oral stories and folklore and through art, drama, and music. Children enter preschool rich in their own language, Cronin emphasized, and effective teaching builds on that strength rather than immersing children in a new language and ignoring the language and literacy development they have experienced so far.

In an English immersion program, Cronin explained to staff, children struggle with learning both basic concepts and language at the same time. She noted that it takes seven years or longer for a person to learn the new academic language, meaning that person speaks, reads, and writes fluently and in grammatically correct ways. In contrast, when a program supports children in learning concepts in their home language, they can more readily transfer these concepts to the second language and actually become fluent in English faster.

The workshop was a success. Teachers spoke with excitement about supporting every child's home language in the classroom. Now we had staff buy-in, but was this enough to bring about the needed change?

We recognized the importance of involving families and the community in the changes we would make. Family services specialists and teachers at each of our centers talked with parents individually and during family-night activities both to educate parents and to invite their feedback. Although initially some parents were hesitant about a dual language approach, as they learned more about language and learning and the benefit to all children, most became strong advocates for dual language and bilingual learning. Bárbara held forums at local schools and community centers to present information to the community at large.

Step 4

Turning Knowledge Into Practice—Experimentation Starts

After the staff training, we noticed that the inconsistencies in classroom support of children's home language began to disappear. Staff knew that the expectations of program leadership had changed. They understood better the importance of supporting children's home language at school and in the home.

In classrooms with bilingual teachers, we observed changes in teaching strategies. Teachers were more intentional in their use of Spanish when conversing with children who were DLLs. At one center, teachers held two circle time groups, one in Spanish and one in English. Children took part in the Spanish circle one day and the English circle the

> Children enter preschool rich in their own language, and effective teaching builds on that strength rather than immersing children in a new language and ignoring the language and literacy development they have experienced so far.

next day, so that both the English and Spanish speakers would experience the same content and activities in each language. Staff requested books for children in Spanish, and we allocated funds to increase our bilingual library. But with all their valiant efforts, staff still expressed frustration and doubt about how to implement a dual language curriculum. Knowledge based primarily on one workshop was not enough to bring about change.

Step 5
Committing Organizational Support

Supporting children's home language is difficult when staff do not speak it. The vast majority of our teaching staff were monolingual English. Many teacher aides or teaching assistants were Spanish speaking, but many had limited English skills. We knew that if children were to hear and converse in their home language, we would need at least one teacher in each classroom who spoke the child's language. In addition to staff training, we changed the ways we support and use language in our classrooms. Our four primary strategies were these:

Hire bilingual staff whenever possible. This was relatively easy for positions that did not require a degree or experience, but we found a very limited, often nonexistent, pool of bilingual applicants for teaching or home-visiting positions that required associate's or bachelor's degrees.

Support monolingual staff in improving their language skills. Our program paid the tuition for several staff members to attend intensive Spanish language classes both during the summer and the school year. This allowed several teaching and home visiting staff, previously uncomfortable conversing in Spanish, to become familiar with the language and able to have meaningful conversations with children and families. Several improved their skills to the point that they no longer needed the support of translators even during parent conferences.

Support bilingual staff in working toward a credential or degree. Our program historically supported center teachers in working toward an AA (associate's) degree in response to national Head Start expectations. We extended that support to aides, many

---

Engaging Families

We divide children into three groups: Spanish, bilingual, and English. We meet with each family and assess the child's needs to determine the primary language. We consider the child's age. If the child will be going to kindergarten next and his English skills are good, we place him in the English group, since kindergarten instruction is in English in our community.

The children learn in their language group during small group and individual activities during choice time. Large group activities are inclusive. The English speakers also learn Spanish. We use props and gestures that help English speakers understand what is happening. Throughout the school year we reassess the children, and we may reassign a child to a different group as needs and skills develop. Teachers also work on their language skills to build their vocabulary in Spanish.

Each year brings something new, so we adjust as needed. Sometimes we have lots of Spanish speakers. Sometimes we have many bilingual Spanish/English. This year one child is becoming trilingual English/Spanish/Punjabi. The mom gave us the Punjabi alphabet and has made labels for the classroom. She also wrote out her child's name in Punjabi so the child could practice writing it each day during sign-in.

Dual language curriculum is a lot of work, but I know that the children and parents are benefiting. Everything we do supports the acquisition of a second language and retention of the primary language. Parents can communicate with the teachers in their language so they can ask questions and participate without any hesitation.

—*Barbara Guillen, Manager,
LaPaloma Head Start Center*

---

of whom were bilingual. After bilingual aides had achieved the CDA (Child Development Associate) credential and/or received AA degrees, they were effective in supporting dual language classroom activities. We created a pool of bilingual candidates ready to apply for teaching positions as these opened up.

Engage language aides. When other strategies were unsuccessful, we found volunteers or hired part-time language aides who worked with children in their home language in the classroom. Teachers reported that having an aide who speaks a child's home language in the classroom even just one hour per day made a difference in a child's ability to integrate into the classroom and maintain his or her home language skills while learning English.

Step 6

Testing New Models in Pilot Centers

With administrative support, staff buy-in, and a growing knowledge and skill base, we readied ourselves to increase the intentional support of home language in the classroom. Four centers expressed a strong interest in piloting an intentional dual language curriculum. Each center's community was completely different, and centers employed staff with skills in different languages. The same approach might not be appropriate for each center, and we knew different models could be effective in supporting bilingual classrooms (Cronin, Lenear, & Sosa Massó 2013).

The mutual support that staff provided to each other was key in encouraging teachers to implement a new and unfamiliar approach.

The models ranged from valuing the home language by learning a few key words and encouraging parents' use of the home language at home to implementing true dual language programs providing meaningful learning experiences and language development in two languages. When determining the best model for a given program, it was important for staff to consider both the language and cultural experiences of enrolled children as well as bilingual language skills of staff.

Bárbara met with each center team to discuss its plans for implementing dual language curriculum. One center, located in a predominantly Latino neighborhood, wanted to teach primarily in Spanish. Even though this was not a true dual language approach, we supported the plan since all the children came from monolingual, Spanish-speaking families. Centers gradually introduced English during the year through small group activities that focused on concepts already learned in Spanish.

Other centers enrolling both English- and Spanish-speaking children assigned part of the day to teaching in Spanish and the balance to teaching in English. Two circle times—one in Spanish and one in English, at different times of the day or on different days and with all children or in small groups—covered the same concepts. Staff who were not fluent in Spanish were encouraged to learn four key words each week to use in conversation with children. One center employed a model that had four days of instruction per week. This included two days teaching in Spanish and two days teaching in English, with the same concepts and activities emphasized in both languages. An Early Head Start class for 2- and 3-year-olds used English one day, Spanish the next day, and sign language on alternate days as a bridge between days.

While many staff understood what they thought a dual language curriculum should look like, a few struggled with program implementation and a concern that if they didn't get it right, children would suffer. Because this concern might hold people back, we encouraged staff to develop their own ideas and strategies. It was important to try and okay to fail and try again. The mentoring and coaching Bárbara provided to center staff was extremely valuable at this stage. She observed in classrooms, scheduled meetings and reflection time with each center team, and arranged for Sharon Cronin to visit each center to observe and offer ideas to staff.

Monthly meetings of the Multicultural Committee became a venue for group sharing and reflection. The support that staff provided to each other was key in encouraging teachers to implement a new and unfamiliar approach. The support from Bárbara and from colleagues helped to ensure that strategies met program expectations.

Step 7

Providing More Staff Development and Experiencing a Little Serendipity

Looking for and taking advantage of opportunities that support change is essential. Our local community college, Skagit Valley College, received a Head Start/Higher Education Latino Partnership Grant. The grant funds let us hire faculty with a strong knowledge of dual language and bilingual curriculum approaches. The award paid the tuition for some staff members to work toward the CDA credential and/or an AA degree. The Early Childhood Education Department of the college arranged a summer, weeklong intensive course in dual language curriculum, led by Sharon Cronin, who had joined the Praxis Institute for Early Childhood Educa-

tion in Seattle. Many of our teaching staff participated and returned to their centers with stronger skills, a fuller understanding of dual language/bilingual curriculum approaches, and a new, positive attitude toward and in support of the program priority for hiring Spanish-speaking staff.

A few months later we experienced another unexpected opportunity that contributed to the success of Skagit/Islands Head Start's changing approach. Six staff members attended the Head Start Latino Institute in Albuquerque. The sessions helped them further build their knowledge and skills, and they met professionals from across the country who were interested in dual language and bilingual curriculum approaches.

Without the grant or the institutes,

we are confident that we would still have been successful in implementing the change to a dual language curriculum. By now we had the commitment of administration, management, and key staff and had accessed resources for building staff knowledge. But this support from outside our program contributed to the effectiveness of dual language learning and to faster adoption of classroom strategies, and it validated the importance of our approach.

Step 8
Reflecting and Planning

Thinking about where you have been and where you are going is crucial to maintaining a paradigm shift and program change. We spent four years developing an understanding of and changing our approach to home language development. We increased the number of bilingual staff in classrooms and furthered staff knowledge and skills about the importance of children learning in their home language. We successfully established an intentional dual language curriculum in several preschool centers, an early Head Start classroom, and a home-visiting program.

In the classroom, areas, materials, and objects are labeled in both Spanish and English (or other language) using one color for each language consistently. We use a new color for labels in each other language. The classroom is full of images, materials, and articles that reflect the children visually, culturally, and linguistically. Small-scale figures for block, sand, and water play look like the children and their extended families (as well as a diversity of other families). The dramatic play area has dolls reflective of the children's cultural and ethnic backgrounds, pretend food that looks like the food eaten by the children and their families, empty containers with labels in the languages of the children, food preparation props from the children's cultural backgrounds, and clothing reflective of what is commonly worn by the children's families. Dramatic play props also introduce children to items used by other cultural groups.

Our new approach is working. Child assessments indicate that children from Spanish-speaking families now demonstrate progress in early literacy skills equal to or better than that of their English-speaking peers. Families understand the importance of their own language to children's learning and value the dual language approach. English- and Spanish-speaking families alike are excited about their children becoming fluent in two languages.

Designing Dual Language Curriculum

Our intention each year is to design a program uniquely responsive to each particular group of children. Decisions about language usage and curriculum choices are based on information gathered from families and observations of the children during the crucial first few weeks of the year.

This year we had a large group of monolingual Spanish speakers. The teaching staff decided to have two teachers in the class speak Spanish and a third teacher speak English throughout the entire day. We recently reassessed the children's needs and, because they are gaining skills in their primary language and developing skills in a second language, we will incorporate more English in our day. This will enable them to practice new terms and phrases in English.

The children have attained language goals more rapidly than in past years when we spoke to them only in English, and this allows us to develop new goals with families. Another benefit we've noticed is an increased sense of community among children in the class.

The journey is not over. There are challenges associated with changing communities and questions yet to be answered. How do we effectively support five or more home languages in the same classroom? With staff turnover, how do we maintain and continue to develop staff knowledge and skills? Without the continued staff development assistance of Bárbara, how do we continue to mentor staff? (Bárbara left to become a full-time instructor at Skagit Valley College.) How do we keep our momentum with increasing demands on our time and attention?

Skagit/Islands Head Start is committed to continuing its efforts to ensure that every child has a strong foundation in his or her home language. Staff from our pilot centers will share what they have learned with other center staff and early childhood professionals in our community. We will collaborate with school district partners who are implementing dual language and bilingual classrooms. We will continue to seek opportunities to increase staff knowledge and skills.

Conclusion

After discovering that Spanish-speaking children in English-immersion preschool classrooms in our Head Start program demonstrated lower literacy and language skills, we transformed our approach to language and learning through an intentional process to

- Increase staff knowledge of language learning and dual language curriculum approaches
- Provide support through bilingual and multicultural materials for children, teachers, and parents, and additional staff when needed
- Increase the number of staff with bilingual skills—through hiring and educating bilingual staff and supporting monolingual staff in pursuing language classes

With encouragement, staff developed and tried new strategies, and the support they received ensured that the strategies met program expectations.

Our efforts were successful. Children from both Spanish- and English-speaking families now demonstrate similar skill levels in language and literacy. Teachers find teaching in a bilingual or dual language classroom very natural. We have participated in the national CRADLE (Cultural Responsiveness and Dual Language Education) project bringing dual language and bilingual learning to Early Head Start. Our Early Head Start teachers implement a trilingual approach with Spanish, English, and American Sign Language.

Update on the Program

As of 2014, Skagit/Islands Head Start has fully integrated dual language instruction into its early Head Start and preschool Head Start centers in communities where a majority of families speak a primary language other than English. Centers with a majority of English speakers also employ some dual language instructional strategies. As new teachers and staff are hired—and every effort is made to hire bilingual teaching and support staff—they receive training on dual language instruction and learning. School districts in the area are also adopting dual language Spanish–English programs, and we have developed strong partnerships with the elementary schools to ensure seamless transitions from our preschool programs into dual language kindergarten programs.

Family advocates help parents understand and value dual language instruction and the importance of a strong foundation in their primary language. In addition to dual language instruction in the classroom, our parent policy council and parent meetings are offered in two languages with simultaneous translation. Dual language instruction at Skagit/Islands Head Start is alive and well.

> With encouragement, staff developed and tried new strategies, and the support they received ensured that the strategies met program expectations.

The future includes maintaining a language-appropriate curriculum approach—dual language or otherwise—in the face of new challenges, including classrooms with multiple languages, and continuing the education of all staff, even in the face of limited funding.

References

Bialystok, E. 2001. *Bilingualism in Development: Language, Literacy, and Cognition.* Cambridge, UK: Cambridge University Press.

Cronin, S., T. Lenear, & C. Sosa Massó. 2013. *Soy Bilingüe: Language, Culture, and Young Latino Children.* Seattle, WA: Center for Linguistic and Cultural Democracy.

Cummins, J. 1992. "Bilingualism and Second Language Learning." *Annual Review of Applied Linguistics* 13: 51–70.

Lee, P. 1996. "Cognitive Development in Bilingual Children: A Base for Bilingual Instruction in Early Childhood Education." *Bilingual Research Journal* 20 (3–4): 499–522.

Makin, L., C. Jones Díaz, & C. McLachlan, eds. 2007. *Literacies in Early Childhood: Changing Views, Challenging Practice.* 2nd ed. Marrickville, NSW: Elsevier Australia.

Quiñones-Eatman, J. 2001. "Preschool Second Language Acquisition: What We Know and How We Can Effectively Communicate With Young Second Language Learners." ED 478930. Technical report #5. Urbana-Champaign, IL: University of Illinois, Early Childhood Research Institute on Culturally and Linguistically Appropriate Services (CLAS).

Sánchez, S., & E. Thorp. 1998. "Policies on Linguistic Continuity: A Family's Right, a Practitioner's Choice, or an Opportunity to Create Shared Meaning and a More Equitable Relationship?" *Zero to Three* 18 (6): 12–20.

Thomas, W.P., & V.P. Collier. 2002. "A National Study of School Effectiveness for Language Minority Students' Long-Term Academic Achievement. Final Report." Project 1.1. Berkeley, CA: University of California–Berkeley Graduate School of Education, Center for Research on Education, Diversity & Excellence. http://crede.berkeley.edu/research/llaa/1.1_final.html.

Karen N. Nemeth
and Pamela
Brillante

naeyc® 2, 3, 7

Supporting Dual Language Learners With Challenging Behaviors

Mrs. Atkins says of 4-year-old Kwan, "Ever since he arrived in my preschool class, I've been at a loss. His parents say Kwan knows some English, but he won't use it with me. The other children stay away from him because they never know when he'll grab their toy or push them. At circle time, he just wanders around the room—no matter what strategies I use to engage him. How do I know if he is acting this way because he doesn't understand us or because he really has some behavior problems? I just don't know what to do!"

I t can be difficult for any teacher to support a child whose behavior is disruptive, but a language barrier can certainly complicate the situation (Santos & Ostrosky 2014). Mrs. Atkins confronts some of the toughest questions facing early childhood educators: How can we distinguish challenging behaviors that are temporary reactions to language differences from those that indicate something else, such as a possible developmental delay or learning disability? And what should we do about it?

Children communicate so much through their behavior. Understanding what their behavior is communicating can be difficult. Children who are new to English may not be able to tell us what's going on. This makes it even more important for teachers to learn specific strategies to interpret children's actions and plan effective interventions.

Factors to Consider

There are no easy answers to these questions. Each dual language learner (DLL) comes with his or her own unique background that includes a variety of experiences and characteristics that can lead to challenging behaviors. In addition to language differences, there may be poverty, stress at home, or upheaval due to the immigration process and moving to a new country with a different culture. The child may have health issues such as allergies or chronic ear infections. Hesitancy or intensity may simply reflect individual personality traits. Even in monolingual children, language development and the ability to communicate can significantly affect behavior. For example, a child with a speech delay might act out due to frustration.

Finding solutions to challenging behaviors in dual language learners is like solving a puzzle because there are so many variables. In this article, we offer some helpful resources and effective strategies that teachers can try right away. To lay the foundation for the approaches suggested in this article, let's consider two important factors.

Over- and Under-Identification

Spanish-speaking children are referred to special education in disproportionately high numbers, especially in schools where home language supports are withdrawn too quickly or not provided at all (Dray 2008). In other cases, dual language learners may be overlooked for special services because language barriers prevent programs from understanding the children's abilities. For children who exhibit challenging behaviors, educators must carefully consider the role of language differences, and the stress they can cause, before making a referral for assessment related to special education support and services. Determinations should be based on multiple measures, focusing on strong observation notes and interviews with parents. Use screening tools and standardized assessments with caution since some commercially available instruments are written only for children who speak English (Espinosa 2010).

Karen N. Nemeth, EdM, is the founder of Language Castle LLC, offering consultation and professional development on first and second language development. She is the author of *Basics of Supporting Dual Language Learners: An Introduction for Educators of Children From Birth Through Age 8* (NAEYC) and other resources for working with young children who are dual language learners.

Pamela Brillante, EdD, is assistant professor of Special Education at the William Paterson University of New Jersey and a consultant in private practice in the areas of early childhood special education and quality inclusive practices.

The Case for Supporting the Home Language

Key findings from research make a clear case for continuing to support young children's home languages while also helping them learn English (Nemeth 2009a). In 2010 the Division for Early Childhood of the Council for Exceptional Children released a revised position statement that addresses this issue with respect to children who have special needs:

> Dual language learners, including those children with disabilities, should be afforded the opportunity to maintain their home language while also learning English as there is no scientific evidence that being bilingual causes or leads to language delay. . . . Supporting a child's home language in fact acts as a linguistic resource and bridge to learning another language, even for children with disabilities. Research confirms that immersing DLLs fully in English when they are still in the active process of learning their home language actually has negative ramifications. (DEC 2010, 5–6)

Types of Challenging Behaviors

Generally, behavior is a form of communication. Children have reasons for engaging in challenging behavior, and it is part of an educator's job to understand what they are trying to express. A child may find that his behavior is effective in getting him something he needs or wants, such as leaving an activity that makes him uncomfortable or getting extra attention from the teacher. It takes time and good detective skills to determine the function of a behavior.

> Children have reasons for engaging in challenging behavior, and it is part of an educator's job to understand what they are trying to express.

Children who are unfamiliar with the language of the classroom may exhibit some of the following behaviors:

◆ Acting out, showing aggression, frustration, anger, or resentment

Three-year-old Carlos, born in Mexico, attends a public school pre-K program. He is still learning his home language and has picked up many new words in English. Carlos enjoys playing alone in the block area, but recently began striking his peers with the blocks. His teacher, Miss Vivian, uses a variety of positive guidance techniques to address this behavior, but Carlos's use of aggression only gets worse. Carlos has now stopped using any of his new English words and is starting to use aggression during other routines and activities during the day. Miss Vivian decides to call on a trusted colleague to help her find more effective solutions for Carlos.

◆ Self-directed signs of stress, such as refusing to eat, having toileting accidents, biting themselves, or pulling their own hair

Parinita, from Sri Lanka, is new to the preschool class. She attempts to join in activities, but rarely seems to smile at mealtimes and eats very little. The teacher notices that there is a lot of table chatter that might make a child who is a DLL feel left out. She introduces the class to key words in Tamil, and the English speakers start paying more attention to their new friend as they practice speaking in her language.

◆ Withdrawal, sadness, isolation, depression, or being mute

Erek and Antoni, 3-year-olds from Poland, are both very quiet in their new American preschool. When their teacher reviews her observation notes, she realizes that neither boy has said a word in school for at least three weeks. Erek's parents report many lively conversations with him at home, so the teacher concludes that he is probably just experiencing a silent period as part of his transition to his new language. She notes that he shows progress in understanding what is said to him in English. Antoni is not only silent but also seems sad. He keeps to himself, at times just rocking back and forth in a chair. He participates very little in class activities, and his parents talk to the teacher about their concern. The teacher and family agree that Antoni seems to need more intensive intervention. The teacher refers him for assessment and he eventually receives special services.

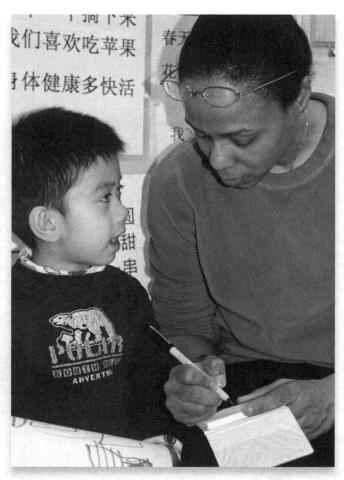

◆ Ignoring directions, being rude or defiant, not listening or participating

From his first day in the program, Jean-Pierre, from France, seems to be in a world of his own. When the other children sit for circle time, he is elsewhere, pulling toys off the shelves. When it is time to dress for outdoor play, Jean-Pierre is busy studying the class pet. When his teacher tries to discuss his behavior with his parents, she realizes they speak little English. Surprised, she double-checks the enrollment form and sees that the family had indicated English as the home language. She realizes that it might have been challenging for the family to accurately complete an English-language form. The teacher vows to make at least one phone call to each new family from now on to confirm the information on the enrollment form.

Any of these behaviors would cause concern in a preschool classroom. Whether caused by language differences or by more complex developmental or situational issues, behavioral problems often indicate that a child is unhappy and not doing well—and teachers want to help. Whatever may be going on with a particular child in distress, unaddressed language differences do not help. The situation creates challenges for teachers, but think about how that young child must feel—dropped off in a strange place for who knows how long with a room full of people he can't understand and who don't understand him.

Even before figuring out what may be causing the child's behaviors, a teacher can begin taking steps to ease the stress of language issues. If it turns out that language is the main cause of the problems, those steps will mean that progress toward improvement is well under way. If other factors are causing the problems, reducing language stress will make it easier for teacher and child to address those factors as well. Providing better language supports and working with the family to help the child deal with the stress of adjustment can result in a gradual decline of the problem behavior. If that doesn't happen, special education or social services may need to provide additional attention. If it seems that the child may have more significant issues, the educator may need to discuss with the family whether to refer the child for assessment. This may lead to a referral to specialists. The local early intervention program or school special education department can help determine if the child is eligible for an Individual Family Service Plan (IFSP) or an Individualized Education Program (IEP), which can include a Functional Behavior Assessment (FBA) and a specific behavior intervention plan.

Prevent Challenging Behaviors Before They Start

Here are some ways to prepare a welcoming environment for each new child.

1. Use a home language survey when each family enrolls, then get further details through meetings or phone conversations about the language(s) that are spoken by the child and family. This is the time to begin building a reciprocal relationship with the family

so you can work as a team to support their child's development and learning.

2. Prepare a list of about 10 to 20 "survival" words or phrases that will help the child feel welcome, safe, and comfortable on his or her first day. (See "Survival Words and Phrases in Spanish and English," p. 48.) Learn the words in each child's language before he or she joins the class.

3. Provide materials that reflect the child's culture and/or are written in the child's home language. These books, puzzles, posters, games, dramatic play props, and music help children see themselves as important members of the community.

Mrs. Murphy recalls how the children's faces lit up when they sang "Feliz Navidad" in December. It made her a little sad that she hadn't prepared to sing a Spanish song with them on their first day so she could have seen those smiles right away.

4. Teach all of the children effective ways to communicate with their classmates who use different languages and have different abilities. Talk about being patient, speaking slowly and repeating, showing their friends what they are talking about, and learning their friends' languages.

Tiffani approaches the newcomer, Andrei, and says slowly, "Hi! My language is English. Do you know English?" When he doesn't respond, she says, "That's OK, my other friend doesn't know my language either." Tiffani takes Andrei's hand and shows him the class pet.

5. Equip your classroom with a picture/symbol communication board (with words) so children can point to items to communicate more effectively.

Observe and Understand Language and Behavior Differences

Skillful and thorough observation is the best way to understand challenging behaviors and develop plans for reducing them. Ask yourself some of the following questions so you can make changes that can help everyone have a better experience.

- ◆ Does the child engage in general and pretend play and interact like other children her age? If not, the challenges may be more developmental than language based.

- ◆ Does the child talk when spending time with another child or staff member who speaks his language? Is he happy and talkative at home? If his language seems on target in some circumstances, you can be sure he does not have a pervasive speech or language delay.

- ◆ Are other children teasing a child because she's different? Teachers need to be sure bullying is not a factor, since it has been observed in children as young as 4, and children who do not speak the majority language are more likely to be victims (Chang et al. 2007).

◆ Is the child silent at school but talking happily when his grandmother comes to pick him up? According to Paradis, Genesee, and Crago (2010), a true language delay or disorder will affect both of the child's languages in about the same way. If there is a lag in only one language, it is generally due to variations in the child's exposure and motivation to learn one language over the other.

◆ Can you detect any particular triggers for the child's challenging behavior, such as large group activities in which she may feel lost and out of place? Changing classroom practice to be more responsive to language differences often results in better experiences for all of the children.

Miss Vivian asks a colleague to help her learn how to chart Carlos's behavior to get the data needed to plan a response. They discover particular situations in which the behavior occurs and then hypothesize that the problem may stem from a language barrier in the class. Miss Vivian decides to develop a common classroom language— using pictures/symbols and words—to help Carlos and his peers communicate. She and her assistant work on facilitating positive interactions among all the children, and they continue to observe and document Carlos's behavior to see if this intervention is working.

Understanding the triggers and results of the behaviors in question allows teachers to help the child learn replacement skills. Was the child really seeking help communicating with his peers? Does it seem that the child is using his behavior to avoid an activity that seems intimidating? It may help to change the activity rather than try to change the child's behavior.

Survival Words and Phrases in Spanish and English

Spanish	English
Hola	Hello
Amigo	Friend
La maestra, el maestro	Teacher
El baño	Bathroom
Comer	Eat
Jugar	Play
Beber	Drink
Lavar	Wash
Tome un descanso.	Take a rest.
¿Necesita ayuda?	Do you need help?
¿Te duele?	Does that hurt?
¡Mucho gusto!	Pleased to meet you!
Tu mama volverá pronto.	Your mom will be back soon.

Adapting Teaching Strategies

Fluctuating populations in early childhood settings require teachers to change their practice. It is not always easy for teachers to give up activities they have used for years, but what worked in the past may not be effective in classrooms that include children with language, behavior, or developmental differences.

Creating a common classroom language adds a visual or kinesthetic component to language. Teachers can provide pictures, symbols, or classroom photographs so children can express themselves when they lack the words or phrases in English. Teachers can also teach some words and phrases in American Sign Language to all children in the classroom. These activities reduce stress by creating a common classroom language that all children can use.

Here are some strategies that can boost the effectiveness of any preschool program that includes children with diverse abilities and language skills:

- ◆ Reduce the use of large group lessons and find more time for small groups and one-on-one interactions throughout the day.

- ◆ Speak slowly, avoid using slang, simplify sentences, and repeat key words often. Be patient, giving children time to process what you've said and respond.

- ◆ Use lots of nonverbal cues—gestures, sign language, facial expression, and changes in voice tone—to enhance communication.

- ◆ Add graphic organizers such as props and pictures that add meaning to interactions.

- ◆ Assign language buddies. If there isn't another child in the class who speaks the same language, encourage a helpful, caring child to befriend the newcomer.

- ◆ Group children who speak the same language during child-directed play times and in large group activities because of the support they can provide both in terms of language practice and social relationships.

- ◆ Provide a comfortable place where a child can spend time playing alone without the constant pressure of trying to understand and be understood.

- ◆ Maintain a predictable schedule. Children may not understand your words, but if a dual language learner knows what's coming next, she is better able to participate appropriately and learn more effectively.

- ◆ Use lots of music and movement activities—in home languages as well as English—to engage all the children while building early language and literacy skills.

- ◆ Make the effort to get to know the families of dual language learners. They can help you make the child more comfortable in the classroom, help you recognize possible signs of trouble, and support your efforts at home. Building a relationship with families will also help you understand how to support them.

- ◆ Develop strong, collaborative relationships with English as a Second Language and bilingual teachers as well as special education professionals and specialists who work with the program. To be most effective, their supports should take the form of consultations with the preschool teacher so he or she can embed and blend their strategies throughout the classroom and throughout the day (Nemeth 2009b).

Engaging Families

Five-year-old Fumiko and her family recently moved from Japan to New Jersey. Wanting to help Fumiko feel comfortable on her first day, Miss Tina, her preschool teacher, purchased some picture books with beautiful illustrations of the mountains and coasts of Japan. On Fumiko's first day, Miss Tina played the Japanese music CDs that she had asked Fumiko's parents to bring in. To Miss Tina's surprise, she did not hear the traditional music she expected and had learned about from old movies. The CDs contained Japanese pop music, the current favorite in Fumiko's home.

Throughout the first week Miss Tina encouraged Fumiko to enjoy the Japanese picture books carefully chosen for her, but she seemed disinterested. When asked about this, Fumiko's mother explained that the family had lived in Tokyo and that the illustrations in the picture books were unfamiliar to her daughter. Miss Tina realized that greeting a new child should not be based on assumptions about a family's culture. To prepare for new children in the future, Miss Tina and her principal decided that teachers would contact each new family and ask them personally about their culture, their interests, and the things the family could add to the classroom that would match their home culture.

It is not always easy for teachers to give up activities they have used for years, but what worked in the past may not be effective in classrooms that include children with language, behavior, or developmental differences.

Conclusion

The strategies that work with dual language learners also can be effective with any child who exhibits challenging behaviors. All of these strategies align with intentional teaching and developmentally appropriate practice. With good teamwork, ongoing professional development, and plenty of patience, helping young dual language learners adjust and succeed can be one of the most rewarding aspects of teaching.

References

Chang, F., G. Crawford, D. Early, D. Bryant, C. Howes, M. Burchinal, O. Barbarin, R. Clifford, & R. Pianta. 2007. "Spanish-Speaking Children's Social and Language Development in Pre-Kindergarten Classrooms." *Early Education and Development* 18 (2): 243–69.

DEC (Division for Early Childhood), Council for Exceptional Children. 2010. "Responsiveness to ALL Children, Families, and Professionals: Integrating Cultural and Linguistic Diversity Into Policy and Practice." Position statement. www.dec-sped.org/uploads/docs/about_dec/position_concept_papers/Position%20Statement_Cultural%20and%20Linguistic%20Diversity_updated_sept2010.pdf.

Dray, B.J. 2008. "Reducing Disproportionality for English Language Learners in Special Education: The Role of Head Start Educators." Head Start English Language Learners Project (HELLP). Podcast transcript. http://headstart.lacoe.edu/userfiles/file/draydisproportionalitypodcastsummary.pdf.

Espinosa, L. 2010. "Assessment of Young English Language Learners." Chap. 7 in *Young English Language Learners: Current Research and Emerging Directions for Practice and Policy,* eds. E. Garcia & E. Frede, 119–42. New York: Teachers College Press.

NAEYC. 2005. "Screening and Assessment of Young English-Language Learners. Supplement to the NAEYC and NAECS/SDE Joint Position Statement on Early Childhood Curriculum, Assessment, and Program Evaluation." www.naeyc.org/files/naeyc/file/positions/ELL_SupplementLong.pdf.

Nemeth, K.N. 2009a. "Meeting the Home Language Mandate: Practical Strategies for All Classrooms." *Young Children* 64 (2): 36–42.

Nemeth, K.N. 2009b. *Many Languages, One Classroom: Teaching Dual and English Language Learners.* Beltsville, MD: Gryphon House.

Paradis, J., F. Genesee, & M.B. Crago. 2010. *Dual Language Development and Disorders: A Handbook on Bilingualism and Second Language Learning.* 2nd ed. Baltimore: Brookes.

Santos, R.M., & M.M. Ostrosky. 2014. "Understanding the Impact of Language Differences on Classroom Behavior." What Works Brief No. 2. Nashville, TN: Center on the Social and Emotional Foundations for Early Learning. Accessed September 25. http://csefel.vanderbilt.edu/briefs/wwb2.pdf.

Meredith K.
Jones and
Pamela L. Shue

Engaging Dual Language Learners in Projects

Excitement over the grand opening of our pizza restaurant—from which we would sell real pizza—mounts as we brainstorm names for our latest project. In a preschool class where the teachers speak only English and the majority of the children speak only Spanish, it is challenging to choose a topic that is interesting enough to engage all children in project work that supports language development. Luckily for the children in my class, pizza is a delicious, familiar, and easily accessible topic to explore. Not only do many of the children have real-life experiences of going to a restaurant to eat pizza with their family, but the school cafeteria serves pizza every Friday and it is a favorite among the children.

I n my (Meredith's) Title I prekindergarten classroom, Spanish is the home language of most of the children. Although everyone's language is valued, the differences can challenge some children. From the beginning of the school year until October, I have noticed that the children whose home language is Spanish play and communicate only with their Spanish-speaking peers. Likewise, the children who speak only English play and talk with their English-speaking peers. Although this is not unexpected, I decided to implement project work to encourage communication between the Spanish speakers and English speakers and language development among all

naeyc 2, 3

the children. It is difficult for dual language learners (DLLs) to learn a new language unless they can engage in social interactions with speakers of the language they are trying to learn (Tabors 2008). Facilitating peer-to-peer communication and social interaction is a common goal of early childhood programs (Mashburn et al. 2009). Our classroom provided the perfect opportunity for the children to engage in social interactions to develop English oral language, increase vocabulary, and enhance social skills.

Projects With Young Dual Language Learners

The Project Approach is a set of teaching strategies implemented to guide children through in-depth, hands-on explorations of real-world topics (Katz & Chard 2000; Helm & Katz 2011). As more classrooms aim to create twenty-first century learners, teachers are finding the Project Approach to be an effective method of delivering curricula while creating opportunities for problem solving, teamwork, and incorporating technology (Bers, New, & Boudreau 2004). Project work can be initiated by the children or the teacher and is based on children's interests, stemming from their life experiences. Projects allow teachers to thoughtfully address specific local or state early learning standards (Helm & Katz 2011). Building on children's interests encourages them to explore meaningful hands-on learning experiences that foster cooperation and responsibility (Dewey [1938] 1997; Helm 2008).

Early in the school year, I introduced the children to this learning process with a teacher-initiated project. Since the majority of children are dual language learners, I began with something familiar to all the children—pizza. Familiar topics help children make connections between prior knowledge and new concepts (Helm 2008). The pizza project provided hands-on learning activities to enhance vocabulary, oral language acquisition, and social skills. I chose the project topic, but the extent of the activities grew from the children's interests.

Meredith K. Jones, MEd, is a doctoral student at the University of North Carolina at Chapel Hill, in the Early Childhood, Special Education, and Literacy program. Meredith's interests include early childhood teacher preparation and developmentally appropriate practices for children who are dual language learners.

Pamela L. Shue, EdD, is an associate professor at the University of North Carolina at Charlotte in the Child and Family Development program. Her work focuses on supporting teachers who work with children and families who are dual language learners and those who live in poverty, as well as issues and policies in prekindergarten.

Getting Started

I introduced the topic through storybooks, beginning with *Hi, Pizza Man!*, by Virginia Walter, and *The Little Red Hen Makes a Pizza!*, by Philemon Sturges. During the read-alouds, I asked the children questions to find out what they knew about pizza (e.g., "What is pizza? Who likes pizza?"). Introducing a project topic to children by using storybooks provides a valuable opportunity to teach new vocabulary and foundational language skills to all children, especially dual language learners (Gaskins & Labbo 2007; Collins 2010). After our readings and discussions, we made a web to document and display what the children knew about pizza, which prompted more questions: "Who works at a pizza restaurant?" and "How do you make pizza?"

To include the dual language learners in this discussion, I wrote a few phrases on chart paper in Spanish and English. *¿Te gusta la pizza?* (Do you like pizza?); *¿Cómo se hace la pizza?* (How do you make pizza?); *¿Qué tipo de pizza te gusta?* (What kind of pizza do you like?). I asked Christine, a child who is bilingual, to translate a few short sentences so the children who spoke Spanish could understand what we were saying. Christine asked them in Spanish if they wanted to make a pizza in our class and eat it. The answer was a loud and encouraging "*¡Sí!*"

During the activities Juan and Maria expressed ideas about an oven to me in Spanish and then showed me what they meant so I could understand. "Oh, you want to make the oven?" I said. "*Muy bien,* very good. *Si,* yes, you can make the oven." The children also talked about eating pizza at home. One child said, "We don't eat there (at the restaurant), we drive and eat it at home." I then questioned if we needed a place to pick up the pizza and a place to sit down and eat. Tommie shared that "Mom and I sit at a table and eat pizza and talk, and you get to drink soda!" "*Mi familia hace pizza en casa. ¡Está caliente!*" exclaimed Pedro. With the help of his peers, Pedro told me his family cooks

pizza at home and it is very hot when it comes out of the oven. The excitement was contagious, and it helped all the children participate in this project.

When we finished our web, the children decided to create what they called "a pizza restaurant" in our classroom so they could make and sell real pizza. To create their vision we had to decide on the different workers needed for the restaurant, learn how to make pizza, and find a way to attract customers. We would also need to role-play all the different aspects of running an actual restaurant so that children would be ready to serve their customers.

To help DLLs make real-world connections, I introduced the children to many new vocabulary words for items we would use in the pizza restaurant (e.g., *pizza pan, pizza cutter, oven, potholder*). Using real-life props, the children helped me verbally identify each item. After naming the prop, I wrote the word in English and Spanish on a sentence strip and attached a picture of the item to help reinforce new vocabulary. These vocabulary words were available to children throughout the day and were often revisited during project work and class meetings.

As our dramatic play center transformed into a pizza restaurant, the children identified tasks and divided them. They decided they needed some children to make the signs and menus, some to build the oven, and others to film the commercial that would air on the school television news. Everyone would write and mail invitations to their friends and families. The dramatic play area now had a table with placemats and a menu, pizza boxes, potholders, napkins, and plates, and the children designated the small play refrigerator to hold the drinks. Two children drew pictures of the school cafeteria's oven to use as a blueprint to build one using a cardboard box. Last, the children placed a cash register and a bowl of sliced fruit for the customers next to the take-out counter.

To ensure the dual language learners were comfortable and engaged as the project unfolded, I implemented role-playing scenarios and continued to model the language by repeating project words and phrases. Specific techniques can foster second language learning, including role-playing and modeling new language (Meier 2004; Tabors 2008; Nemeth 2009). During our role-playing sessions, each child portrayed a restaurant worker and a customer. Our sessions took place every day during the second week of the

To help DLLs make real-world connections, I introduced the children to many new vocabulary words for items we would be using in the pizza restaurant.

project and let all the children have hands-on experiences with props such as pizza pans and boxes. They learned how to write customers' orders on a small notepad, how to use a spatula to put a piece of pizza on a plate, how to clear the table after customers are done eating, and how to give customers their bill. These sessions provided rich English language modeling for the Spanish-speaking children, and role-playing with props helped all the children understand how to use them correctly.

To provide opportunities for dual language learners and English-speaking children to work together, we created small groups that reflected children's job preferences. Each day during our morning meeting, I announced four jobs that had been suggested by the children to create our restaurant (e.g., making the menus, creating the grand opening signs, building the oven, and making the placemats). Each group had four job openings to ensure the groups were equal and that every child had a job. I also explained what each job entailed and showed the children the materials they could use to complete their job. Next, I asked the children one by one which job they wanted to sign up for. To encourage group diversity I alternated between calling on English speakers and Spanish speakers, as well as between girls and boys. This system of creating our small groups continued throughout the entire project.

While supporting the small groups, the classroom assistant and I used several communication techniques to provide meaningful feedback and to model new language, including talking slowly, using gestures and hand motions, using repetition, and expanding and extending what children were discussing (Massey 2004; Tabors 2008).

At morning meeting time, each group told the class what they had accomplished the previous day and what their plans were for that day. During this sharing, we made sure everyone agreed on their goals and who would work together. I asked the children specific higher-level questions (see "Project Questions," p. 56) to facilitate conversations and improve their critical thinking (Yamauchi et al. 2012). Answering higher-level questions is challenging, as it requires children to process what they already know, then expand on their prior knowledge to answer the question. For DLLs, this process has an additional step of translating their previous knowledge in their home language to the new language and then producing the answer in the new language (Meier 2004; Tabors 2008). As the children answered the higher-level questions and explained their work to the class, they were all able to practice their English oral language skills, use new vocabulary, demonstrate the pride they had in their work, and come together as a democratic community to further the project.

Involving All Families

> A benefit of using project work with children learning a second language is the increased level of parental involvement in classrooms. Parents of second-language learners can contribute to the project by providing needed materials from home and sharing home vocabulary for words related to the project. (Helm & Beneke 2003, 70)

Before the project began, I sent a newsletter home with the children to inform families and invite them to participate in our pizza project, which would take place over two weeks. The newsletter explained the purpose of the project and its three main objectives: (1) the children would learn new vocabulary words (the newsletter included the Spanish and English words), (2) the activities would increase opportunities for the children to develop their oral language skills to support future literacy success, and (3) the process would support development of children's social interactions, which would strengthen problem-solving skills and create new friendships.

During the project a few Spanish-speaking parents visited our class to help children in their work and offer assistance in Spanish when needed. One parent who owns a grocery store in our community provided ingredients to make the pizzas. Several of the ingredients had Spanish labels, and the children recognized them from their own homes. The families' involvement during the project strengthened the relationship between home and classroom.

Engaging Families

Invo ving families in our class projects is one of my main goals as a teacher. Sometimes I face a language challenge because I do not speak Spanish and many of the families speak primarily Spanish at home. During our pizza project I sent out weekly newsletters in English and Spanish inviting families to donate ingredients for the pizzas. One morning a father who owned a local *tienda* (store) arrived carrying two bags full of ingredients. Without the use of a translator it was difficult for us to talk, but we were able to communicate. Beaming from ear to ear, he showed me the list of ingredients and motioned that it was all in the bags. His expression conveyed his feeling that he was making a valuable contribution to the classroom and to his daughter's education. A few days later the school translator told me about a conversation he had had with this father. The father had shared that by bringing in ingredients from his *tienda* he felt like he was able to participate in class activities. He no longer felt uncomfortable because of the language barrier. This experience strengthened our relationship with this father and reminded me of the many ways I can encourage parents to become involved in the classroom!

"Welcome to Pizzería!"

After the children sent invitations to friends, family, and school personnel, and the school librarian had broadcast the children's commercial throughout the school, the children were ready to practice their jobs. Again, the children selected the job they wanted and I made sure the groups included both Spanish and English speakers. Next, teachers watched the groups role-play, rehearsing the different phrases they would need to use when customers came to the pizza restaurant. The role-playing helped to build the children's confidence.

Next, as a whole group we made the pizzas to sell to customers. Again, I showed the children all the ingredients we needed, and we made a how-to list of steps to follow when making a pizza. Once we made our list, I invited each child to help me prepare the pizzas for the cafeteria oven. After we cooked the pizzas, we discussed how they were very hot and needed to be sliced. The children watched as I sliced the pizzas and wrapped each slice in aluminum foil to keep it warm. Next, we decided how to label the slices with pepperoni. The children agreed that we could put a red dot on their labels. After labeling all the slices, we moved them to the children's cardboard oven where they would wait to be sold.

As the customers entered the classroom they received $4.00 of play money to pay for their meal. "Welcome to Pizzería! Would you like to dine in or take out?" The waiter greeted our first customer and showed her to the table. "Here is your menu. We have pizza and drinks. What would you like to eat?" The children quickly realized they weren't playing anymore—this was a real job and they had to work together to run their pizza restaurant. A dual language learner took the first customer's order using the new words ("Cheese or pepperoni pizza?") and then asked, "Would you like to drink juice or water?" He took the customer's order and relayed it to the English-speaking cook. While the waiter got the customer's water, the cook carefully placed a slice of cheese pizza on a plate and gave it to the customer.

Project Questions

Basic Level Questions

1. Do you like pizza?
2. Where do you eat pizza?
3. What kind of pizza do you like?
4. How do you make a pizza?

Mid Level Questions

5. In what way might you tell people the pizza restaurant is open?
6. What would be a good name for our restaurant?
7. How would you use the information you learned about starting a pizza restaurant to start something else?
8. What is the order of how you mix the ingredients to make the pizza dough?

Upper Level Questions

9. What would happen if we did not tell people about the pizza restaurant?
10. What was the most important part of the pizza restaurant?
11. How well did you do running the pizza restaurant?
12. What would happen if the oven did not work?

On the first day our restaurant was open it was important to assist the children when needed, reminding them what to say to the customers and how to perform their role. I watched for frustration or signs they were overwhelmed. For some children, regardless of the language they speak, talking to unfamiliar adults and remembering what to say and do can be difficult. When a child decided she did not want to work anymore, the next child who signed up for that job took over.

On the second and final day of business, the children were more comfortable and ready for the customers. They needed fewer reminders of what to do and say, and ran their restaurant without help from the teachers. The children's pizza restaurant was a success, and to celebrate they cooked their own pizza and enjoyed the results of their efforts.

What We Learned

As the children worked hard at the pizza restaurant, I documented behaviors in the following categories: (1) social interactions between English- and Spanish-speaking children, (2) vocabulary words used and whether they were used appropriately, (3) how often dual language learners used English words and phrases related to the project work, and (4) how the children showed pride in their work.

As I observed, Jonathan quickly placed an order to Ana and said, "I need two pieces of pizza (holding up two fingers) from the oven (pointing to the oven). And the customer wants water to drink." After getting the pizza ready, Ana opened the refrigerator and grabbed a bottle of water, then asked Jonathan, "¿Agua?" Jonathan replied, "Yes, agua. Water." From this brief exchange it was clear the children were communicating well as a team to accomplish their job.

A few customers later, Christine scribbled a customer's order on her notepad and handed it to Alejandro, the cashier. As the customer waited to pay for his bill, Christine reminded Alejandro what to say. With Christine's help, Alejandro assertively exclaimed to the customer, "You pay four dollars and I give you the pizza and a drink!" After the customer paid his bill, Christine and Alejandro announced in unison, "Thank you for coming! _¡Adios!_" While watching this, I noticed that Christine helped her Spanish-speaking peer use the English phrases we had practiced, and gave him a boost of confidence by encouraging him to say them aloud. The confidence and certainty the children demonstrated made it clear how much they valued their pizza restaurant and how quickly they began to acquire a new language.

Reflecting on the pizza project, I examined my notes, photographs, and video recordings. From these resources I found that the social interactions among the dual language learners and English speakers had developed from teacher-initiated to child-initiated. The children had gained confidence in communicating with each other to solve problems and continued to use the new vocabulary correctly during the project. Although their English oral language skills are continuing to develop, the dual language learners appear to be much more comfortable speaking English to teachers and their English-speaking peers. These observations are vital in determining future project work.

Conclusion

On the last day of the pizza project I overheard a teacher who had been a customer at our restaurant say, "I can't believe 4- and 5-year-olds are doing this. They put a lot of hard work into making their restaurant and they are really making it work!" I was proud of the children and all they accomplished. They continue to work together to overcome language barriers, learn new skills, and support one another to make their ideas real. By all accounts, this project was a huge success. The children enjoyed this way of learning, and we now are embarking on a _child-initiated_ project: The Book Store!

References

Bers, M.U., R.S. New, & L. Boudreau. 2004. "Teaching and Learning When No One Is Expert: Children and Parents Explore Technology." _Early Childhood Research and Practice_ 6 (2).

Collins, M.F. 2010. "ELL Preschoolers' English Vocabulary Acquisition from Storybook Reading." _Early Childhood Research Quarterly_ 25 (1): 84–97.

Dewey, J. [1938] 1997. _Experience and Education_. New York: Touchstone.

Gaskins, I.W., & L.D. Labbo. 2007. "Diverse Perspectives on Helping Young Children Build Important Foundational Language and Print Skills." _Reading Research Quarterly_ 42 (3): 438–51.

Helm, J.H. 2008. "Got Standards? Don't Give Up on Engaged Learning." _Young Children_ 63 (4): 14–20. www.naeyc.org/files/yc/file/200807/BTJJudyHarrisHelm.pdf.

Helm, J.H., & S. Beneke, eds. 2003. _The Power of Projects: Meeting Contemporary Challenges in Early Childhood Classrooms—Strategies and Solutions_. New York: Teachers College Press; Washington, DC: NAEYC.

Helm, J.H., & L.G. Katz. 2011. _Young Investigators: The Project Approach in the Early Years_ 2nd ed. New York: Teachers College Press; Washington, DC: NAEYC.

Katz, L.G., & S.C. Chard. 2000. _Engaging Children's Minds: The Project Approach_. 2nd ed. Stamford, CT: Ablex.

Mashburn, A.J., L.M. Justice, J.T. Downer, & R.C. Pianta. 2009. "Peer Effects on Children's Language Achievement During Pre-Kindergarten." _Child Development_ 80 (3): 686–702.

Massey, S.L. 2004. "Teacher–Child Conversation in the Preschool Classroom." _Early Childhood Education Journal_ 31 (4): 227–31.

Meier, D.R. 2004. _The Young Child's Memory for Words: Developing First and Second Language and Literacy_. New York: Teachers College Press.

Nemeth, K.N. 2009. _Many Languages, One Classroom: Teaching Dual and English Language Learners_. Lewisville, NC: Gryphon House.

Tabors, P.O. 2008. _One Child, Two Languages: A Guide for Early Childhood Educators of Children Learning English as a Second Language_. 2nd ed. Baltimore: Brookes.

Yamauchi, L.A., S. Im, C.-J. Lin, & N.S. Schonleber. 2012. "The Influence of Professional Development on Changes in Educators' Facilitation of Complex Thinking in Preschool Classrooms." _Early Child Development and Care_ 185 (5): 689–706.

Iliana Alanís

Where's Your Partner? Pairing Bilingual Learners in Dual Language Classrooms

Teachers commonly separate children to work on their own, using phrases like, "I want to see what *you* can do, not your neighbor" or "Work quietly on your own." Children working alone is a common instructional strategy in some early childhood classrooms (Alanís 2011). According to foundational work by Johnson and Johnson (1986), however, cooperative teams employ higher levels of thought and retain information longer than children who work individually. Children engage in discussion, take responsibility for their learning, and become critical thinkers when they work and learn together. To develop a first or second language, children need to hear language in rich and meaningful contexts that help them connect what they are learning with

their prior experiences. They also need opportunities to practice their oral and written language skills. When dual language learners collaborate, often in a nondominant language, they use their language skills in natural conversations as they develop an understanding of academic concepts.

As dual language programs increase in number, teachers are changing the way they teach, based on the characteristics of the children in the class and the goals of the program. As a professional development provider and associate professor, I have worked with early childhood dual language teachers in Spanish/English programs at various stages, from the first to the fifth year of implementation. Each requires its own level of support and professional development. I've seen how teachers organize instruction and adjust their teaching styles to enhance program goals for Spanish and English academic development. For example, effective teachers integrate visuals and graphics into the lesson to facilitate understanding for dual language learners. They also focus on helping children develop content understanding by providing more hands-on instruction and concrete examples.

Bilingual Pairs: Increasing Linguistic and Academic Development

Pairing bilingual children is an effective cooperative learning strategy in Spanish/English dual language classrooms (Alanís 2011). Teachers assess children's linguistic and academic proficiency levels and pair them *heterogeneously*—that is, they pair children with higher skill levels with partners whose skills are less developed. Thus, children are mixed by varying levels of understanding and oral language skills. Pairs are the ideal group size for cooperative language learning because they ensure more opportunities for children to participate than typically occur in small or whole group instruction. Pairs also maximize practice opportunities for purposeful, extended talk. Children can participate at least half of the time in well-constructed activities.

Learning is social. Working in bilingual pairs drives language and concept development, provides opportunities to develop more complex language patterns of talk, and builds linguistic confidence in a fun, relaxing environment (DePalma 2011). Adults or more competent peers support children's development through interactions within a social context known as the *zone of proximal development*. As conceived by Vygotsky (1978), the zone of proximal development helps the learner achieve tasks with the aid of a more competent person, such as a skilled classmate, an older child, or a teacher. Cooperative learning through bilingual pairs creates social and linguistic interactions where the teacher and the bilingual partners provide assistance and direction, and where children learn new behaviors and skills in collaboration with others (Bodrova & Leong 2005).

Encouraging cooperative learning with bilingual pairs is a natural way to create a community of learners in which children feel comfortable and connected to those around them (Riojas-Cortez & Flores 2009). Children are more willing to take risks as learners when they feel they can make mistakes without negative repercussions (Church 2004). Additionally, bilingual pairs reinforce native speakers' knowledge of their home language and demonstrate respect for the minority language and culture (García 2005). These feelings of pride and self-esteem help children build an important base for their further success in school.

Teachers of dual language learners can pair children throughout the day using a variety of cooperative learning strategies. The following bilingual pairing strategies are easy to implement on a regular basis and can be adapted to any classroom setting. They allow children to express themselves in meaningful and nonthreatening contexts and challenge each other's ideas as they engage in conversations about concepts found in the academic curriculum.

Tell Your Partner: Turn-and-Talk

An important part of an early childhood program is circle time, a scheduled, adult-led group with children seated on the carpet, often with a focus on children's language and concept development. Whole group settings can be an effective learning context where

Iliana Alanís, PhD, is an associate professor in the Department of Interdisciplinary Learning and Teaching for the University of Texas at San Antonio. Her work focuses on teaching practices in early elementary, with an emphasis on the effect of schooling for language minority children in bilingual programs. Dr. Alanís is a former president of the Texas Association for Bilingual Education, has numerous publications in the area of dual language education, and has facilitated professional development for multiple levels of education.

> Encouraging cooperative learning with bilingual pairs is a natural way to create a community of learners where children feel comfortable and connected to those around them.

children can express themselves, hear the opinions of others, and feel part of the larger learning community (Bredekamp 2013). The concept of turn-and-talk provides a space for children to physically turn and talk to their partner. When children use turn-and-talk, they converse among themselves. The teacher hears more responses because all children are engaged in a conversation.

> Mrs. Salinas, a Spanish/English kindergarten teacher, gathers the children on the carpet. She initiates a discussion about families by giving a verbal prompt: *Dile a tu, vecino quienes son los miembros de tu familia.* (Tell your neighbor who are the members of your family.) The children physically turn their bodies to face the child sitting next to them and begin to talk about their families. Most of the children choose to speak in their home language, the language they are most comfortable with. After two minutes, Mrs. Salinas asks a few children to share with the class. *¿Rodrigo, que dijo McKayla de su familia?* (Rodrigo, what was McKayla saying about her family?) By asking Rodrigo to tell the group about McKayla's family, Mrs. Salinas focuses on his listening comprehension as well as his oral language development.

During the turn-and-talk activity, the children practice their language skills and talk about their families—a meaningful topic of conversation for them. The activity gives the teacher information about each child's home life, which she can use in developing future activities (Riojas-Cortez & Flores 2009). Throughout the activity, she asks questions while informally assessing children's responses for concept understanding.

Teachers can use the turn-and-talk strategy to

- Tap into children's prior knowledge before beginning an activity or study
- Develop KWL (what I **K**now, what I **W**ant to know, what I **L**earned) charts as the activity proceeds
- Review information throughout the activity
- Brainstorm ideas throughout the activity
- Check for understanding throughout the activity
- Summarize understandings at the end of the activity

I have observed successful use of the turn-and-talk strategy in bilingual classrooms from prekindergarten to second grade. Children seem to enjoy it because it allows them to talk and learn with other children in an informal and fun way (DePalma 2011).

Tell Your Partner: Think-Pair-Share

Whole group activities are also an appropriate time for teachers to use the think-pair-share strategy (Lyman 1981). Think-pair-share engages children in a short amount of time by first providing a few minutes for children to think about what they want to say and then encouraging them to share their thoughts with their partner.

> Ms. Oliva, a bilingual Spanish/English first grade teacher, asks the children to think about a previous science lesson on living organisms and nonliving objects. She says they will think silently before responding, and then states, "Think of two things that are living and two things that are nonliving." Ms. Oliva's prompt lets the children reflect on what they already know about the concept of living and nonliving and connect it to their personal lives by talking about things they have experience with or know about.
>
> After a minute or so, the children choose a partner and share their answers. Although the lesson is in English, they can answer in their home languge. After a few more min-

utes, she asks partners to be prepared to share one example and its characteristics with the group. Using this brainstorming strategy, children quickly negotiate with each other which examples to share. As they explain the different characteristics of living organisms and nonliving objects, the children practice their science vocabulary. This strategy allows classmates to hear others' ideas and compare them with their own.

When teachers pause between asking a question and soliciting a response, they give children time to think about their response and organize their thoughts. During the early stages of second language acquisition, children silently translate the question to their home language, think of the answer, and then translate it back to the language of the teacher. The wait time afforded in think-pair-share gives all children a chance to be successful.

The think-pair-share strategy has several advantages for teachers because it

◆ Doesn't take much preparation time

◆ Engages the entire class in a short amount of time

◆ Allows the teacher to ask different levels of questions and assess children's understanding by listening in on several groups during the activity and collecting responses at the end

Think-pair-share offers several advantages for learning because

◆ Children who tend to be quiet are more likely to answer questions in a smaller group, which can reduce their anxiety about speaking in front of an audience or large group

◆ Children encourage and support each other's use of language

◆ Children engage in real-life, authentic interactions as they reinforce their academic language

Teachers need to ask open-ended questions that encourage thinking rather than questions with one right answer (Alanís 2011). Children need to engage in academic conversations to have the experience and knowledge to challenge each other's ideas and develop their own perspectives.

Work With Your Partner: Hands-on Activities

As mentioned previously, the nature of classroom activities affects the quantity and quality of children's talk. Teachers who use strategies that encourage children to engage with each other create very different environments than teachers who expect children to sit quietly throughout most of the lesson. For example, the activity described below integrates literacy and science learning. It enables children to practice their speaking and writing skills and their academic vocabulary.

Ms. Oliva then asks the first-graders to go back to their tables and work with their partners to continue their study of living and nonliving objects. She gives each pair a bag of photos and a T-chart. This sheet of paper has a graphic organizer in the shape of a large T, which creates two columns. The columns are labeled at the top with the categories *Living* and *Nonliving*. Ms. Oliva tells the children, "Name each object and discuss where to place the object on the chart—living or nonliving. Explain why the object goes under that heading. If your partner does not agree, he or she must explain why. Then decide whether your partner is correct or you are correct, based on the characteristics of living organisms."

The children discuss each item with their partners before deciding which category to place their object in. Children correct each other when necessary, and they also confirm each other's understandings. For example, Mario reminds Parker that "snails are alive but they live inside a shell."

Once the children complete the activity, Ms. Oliva asks some of the partners to report their findings to their classmates. Finally, she asks all of the children to write a summary of their learning in their science journals and then read the entry to their partner. Although Parker struggled earlier in the lesson, by the time he writes down his understandings in his journal he has a better idea of the concept and has had time to discuss his ideas with Mario.

Ms. Oliva gave the children only one set of materials so that they had to work together. She gave clear directions and expectations for the assignment. Children need such clarity and the teacher's active involvement to reap the benefits of working with peers. When children receive materials and clear guidance on how to work with their partners, they complete the assignment together and can clarify their understandings and solidify new knowledge.

Work With Your Partner: Learning Centers

Well-stocked learning centers—such as blocks, dramatic play, and discovering science—are powerful tools to develop children's language, cognition, and problem solving and social skills (Epstein 2014). They provide a child-initiated setting for meeting the diverse learning needs and interests of young children (Morrison 2010). When children play and work in learning centers with a partner, they can refine key concepts, apply conceptual and linguistic knowledge, and integrate speaking and listening in a relaxed and enjoyable environment (Bredekamp 2011).

In some early childhood bilingual classrooms, teachers heterogeneously partner children at centers based on their varying linguistic and academic developmental levels to do teacher-created activities together. The activities require children to engage in conversations about the content or concepts. Some activities are a review of previous concepts, others reinforce study unit concepts, and yet others extend the children's skills in certain content areas.

In the math center of Mr. Luna's bilingual prekindergarten classroom, pairs of children practice one-to-one correspondence. Mr. Luna provides bags filled with Popsicle sticks, one for each pair. Each stick has dots or numbers painted on it. The goal is for children to count the dots on one Popsicle stick and find the corresponding number on another Popsicle stick.

At circle time, Mr. Luna introduces the activity and shows children what they will do. He demonstrates by using the word *match* often and counting slowly so children will understand. He then asks two children to come up to the front and model for their classmates. They take turns counting and matching Popsicle sticks with corresponding dots. As they model, Chris tells Doreen, his partner, who has matched three dots with the number four Popsicle stick: "That only has three dots." At first Doreen looks puzzled, but soon realizes her error and adjusts. She smiles and says, "I knew that." Chris seems satisfied with her answer. They go on until all Popsicle sticks have been matched.

Children learn a great deal from doing learning center activities with their bilingual partners. The children's cooperation leads to peer-mediated instruction and the development of academic language. Center activities build children's knowledge and engage them in small, extended conversations that require complex language skills rather than one-word answers. Working with a partner at centers predisposes children to help each other and creates a safe environment in which they can learn together. In other words, children are used to the process, understand the expectation, and feel comfortable in their learning.

Ways to Partner Children

In dual language classrooms, it's best to partner children based on varying language skills and cognitive ability. When teachers include various activities using partners, children understand their partnerships are flexible. They may have different partners for different content areas. A good partnering for language arts, for example, might not be effective for mathematics, depending on children's numeracy skills. As children gain linguistic or academic proficiency, teachers can rearrange pairs to maintain their heterogeneity, with the help of moveable management plans, such as Velcro-backed or magnetic name labels or color-coded pocket charts. These charts also tell children who to sit next to once the activity begins, making transitions smoother.

Helping Pairs Learn to Work Together

Young children are learning to share, take turns, and show caring behaviors for others. Structured activities that promote cooperation can help children build these social skills. The two most important words when it comes to children working together are *structure* and *consistency* (Alanís 2011). Many children require explicit modeling and time for role-playing before beginning to work in pairs. In addition, guided practice is crucial. It lets the teacher assess if children understand the expectation and adjust when necessary before having them do the activity on their own. Teachers can establish routines so that children understand what to do and how to manage themselves.

The most effective way to teach children to engage with a partner is to role-play with them. Demonstrate what working with a partner sounds like and looks like. Also effective is to show them what working with a partner does not look like. Sometimes children enjoy watching adults act out unacceptable behaviors in a playful way. Teachers can overdramatize resistance to sharing or can be overly dramatic about not wanting to take turns. Adults and children can then discuss the positive way to learn with a partner by sharing and taking turns. Role-playing can be done with a paraprofessional, parent, or another child. Having children role-play partnering several times before they work together helps them work together more effectively and reduces the need for teacher mediation.

Conclusion

When developing activities, dual language teachers need to decide when to have children partner and talk to each other. Bilingual pairing works best when children partner before, during, and at the end of the activity (Alanís 2011). This means children are engaging with each other throughout the lesson, not just during practice time or as a closure. The more children engage in conversations about what they know and what they are learning, the more comfortable they feel with each other and the more relaxed they will feel about the learning process itself.

In supportive learning environments children have meaningful language experiences that are cognitively and linguistically stimulating (Neuman et al. 2007). Bilingual pairing lets children share ideas and practice their oral language skills without being afraid of making mistakes. Working together is a powerful way for children to learn and meet some of the social and cognitive demands of their lives in and out of school. More important, it validates children's home language and communicates to all children that they have important ideas to share and that they are capable of meaningful conversation and learning.

References

Alanís, I. 2011. "Learning From Each Other: Bilingual Pairs in Dual Language Classrooms." *Dimensions of Early Childhood* 39 (1): 21–28.

Bodrova, E., & D.J. Leong. 2005. "Uniquely Preschool." *Educational Leadership* 63 (1): 44–47.

Bredekamp, S. 2013. *Effective Practices in Early Childhood Education: Building a Foundation.* 2nd ed. New York: Pearson.

Church, E.B. 2004. "Group Time: Creating a Community of Learners." *Early Childhood Today* 19 (3): 54–55.

DePalma, R. 2011. *Language Use in the Two-Way Classroom: Lessons From a Spanish-English Bilingual Kindergarten.* Bristol, UK: Multilingual Matters.

Epstein, A.S. 2014. *The Intentional Teacher: Choosing the Best Strategies for Young Children's Learning.* 2nd ed. Washington, DC: NAEYC; Ypsilanti, MI: HighScope Press.

García, E.E. 2005. *Teaching and Learning in Two Languages: Bilingualism and Schooling in the United States.* New York: Teachers College Press.

Johnson, R.T., & D.W. Johnson. 1986. "Action Research: Cooperative Learning in the Science Classroom." *Science and Children* 24 (2): 31–32.

Lyman, F.T. 1981. "The Responsive Classroom Discussion: The Inclusion of All Students." In *Mainstreaming Digest,* ed. A.S. Anderson, 109–13. College Park: University of Maryland Press.

Morrison, G.S. 2010. *Fundamentals of Early Childhood Education.* 6th ed. New Jersey: Pearson.

Neuman, S.B., K. Roskos, T. Wright, & L. Lenhart. 2007. *Nurturing Knowledge: Building a Foundation for School Success by Linking Early Literacy to Math, Science, Art, and Social Studies.* New York: Scholastic.

Riojas-Cortez, M., & B.B. Flores. 2009. "Supporting Preschoolers' Social Development in School Through Funds of Knowledge." *Journal of Early Childhood Research* 7 (2): 185–99.

Vygotsky, L.S. 1978. *Mind in Society: The Development of Higher Psychological Processes.* Cambridge, MA: Harvard University Press.

Karen N. Nemeth and Fran S. Simon

Using Technology as a Teaching Tool for Dual Language Learners

Miss Jessie raises her hand at the teacher workshop. She tells the other participants, "I was hired because I am bilingual, but then they put me in a class where most of the children don't speak English or my home language, which is Spanish. I walked into my first day of teaching preschool faced with 18 bright, adorable children who speak Arabic, Korean, or Polish most of the time. Where do I start?"

Miss Jessie's concern is not unique. Early childhood educators across the United States are asking similar questions. Teachers often report that they have three, four, or more languages in their classroom—and those languages change from year to year. To add to the challenge, multilingual materials can be hard to find and costly. It is important for teachers to have as many tools as possible to help them meet the language needs of all children in this ever-changing landscape.

In addition to books and other materials in your classroom, technology tools allow you to find multilingual resources and create activities and materials that can be adapted quickly and inexpensively to meet changing language needs. There are also software applications (apps) for your computer, phone, or other electronic devices and interactive websites that can support children's dual language experiences. In this article, we describe ways to use the technology you might already have and offer some new ideas to inspire you.

Challenging Common Myths About DLLs

New strategies for teaching young children who are dual language learners should support academic learning in each child's home language within a cultural context while also supporting English learning (p. 20).

Karen N. Nemeth, EdM, is the founder of Language Castle LLC, offering consultation and professional development on first and second language development. She is the author of *Basics of Supporting Dual Language Learners: An Introduction for Educators of Children From Birth Through Age 8* (NAEYC) and other resources for working with young children who are dual language learners.

Fran S. Simon, MEd, an early childhood consultant, works with organizations and companies in technology development, advocacy, and business development. She is the coauthor of *Digital Decisions: Choosing the Right Technology in Early Childhood*.

Photos courtesy of United Way Center for Excellence in Early Education, Miami, Florida

Technology Appears in Many Forms

Whether you use simple technology like CD or DVD players, MP3 players, or digital cameras, or more complex tools like interactive whiteboards (IWBs), you can put technology to work to enhance your teaching practices. A good place to start is taking stock of what is available to you right now. Check the items you already have in your classroom.

- ❏ Digital camera/video camera
- ❏ Device to record children's language
- ❏ Internet access
- ❏ Tablet
- ❏ Interactive whiteboard
- ❏ Smartpen or digital pen
- ❏ Music player
- ❏ Laptop or desktop computer
- ❏ Smartphone
- ❏ Printer
- ❏ Multitouch table or smart table
- ❏ Video monitor

These commonly available technology tools can be powerful assets for working with children in your classroom, especially with dual language learners (DLLs). Careful, intentional planning will help you make the most of the technology you choose to use and ensure that your choices fit your curriculum goals. Matching your technology resources to the needs of adults and children in your class and families at home will be the basis for your technology planning in a multilingual environment.

The Basics

Once you have determined which technology tools are available, consider other elements you need in your classroom to support DLLs. Several items on the "Ready for Dual Language Learners" classroom checklist from *Basics of Supporting Dual Language Learners* can be facilitated using technology:

- ❏ Staff members are aware of each child's home language and country of origin.
- ❏ All of the children's languages and cultures are represented in the classroom.
- ❏ The classroom has audio recordings of a few key welcoming words in each child's language.
- ❏ Classroom signs and labels are written with phonetic spellings in different languages.
- ❏ Outdoor play area has picture and written labels, and safety messages in English and the children's home languages. (Nemeth 2012, 35–36)

You can find suggestions about using technology appropriately to support DLLs in the joint position statement from NAEYC and the Fred Rogers Center for Early Learning and Children's Media (NAEYC & Fred Rogers Center 2012), including the following highlights:

- ◆ "Technology tools can be effective for dual language learners by providing access to a family's home language and culture while supporting English language learning." (9)
- ◆ It is our responsibility to do our part to ensure equitable access for all children and all families.

These ideas for using technology to bridge language barriers in early childhood education might broaden your view of how you can use technology to meet the needs of all children in your classroom, including DLLs.

Many early childhood educators in the United States are not bilingual. Even those who are might not work in classrooms in which the children speak the languages the teacher speaks (like Miss Jessie in our opening vignette). Still, all early childhood teachers can provide some level of home language support that honors and respects the unique background and identity of each child and lets children build on the knowledge they have gained in that home language. Your efforts to support home language learning will benefit all the children in the classroom by building cultural and linguistic bridges to help them communicate in an increasingly global society.

Early childhood programs address home language support in different ways, based on the needs of the families they serve, the abilities of their staff, the curriculum and requirements they must address, and the resources they have available. Technology can help you juggle all of these factors, but it is not a one-size-fits-all answer. "For technology to be developmentally appropriate, it should be responsive to the ages and developmental levels of the children, to their individual needs and interests, and to their social and cultural contexts" (McManis & Gunnewig 2012, 6). Technology is just one of many tools that can be used effectively in the hands of an intentional and planful early childhood teacher. It shouldn't replace the great things already happening in your classroom, but it can enhance and improve teaching and learning experiences when used for a specific purpose. Electronic enhancements are especially powerful for DLLs.

Whether you speak one language or many, technology can help you reach all the children in your classroom. A national survey completed in 2012 by the Early Childhood Technology Collaborative (www.ecetech.net) found that more than half of responding early childhood educators and leaders said they use technology to support DLLs.

Uses of Technology

Here are a number of ideas for using technology to support dual language learners.

Adapt or Create Materials to Work for DLLs

◆ Try translation software such as Google Translate, or iTranslate on mobile devices, to help you find and learn key words in the children's home languages. This can help you communicate and begin integrating languages throughout your learning centers. Using these tools, you can print out words and phrases to make books, games, or activities written in English more accessible for all the children. Tablets and smartphones put those translation capabilities at your fingertips (Simon & Nemeth 2012). Use caution with translation apps—a computer may not always provide the appropriate words for the message you want to communicate.

◆ Use a digital camera to capture photos and videos of things in the environment that are familiar to the children. Using recognizable photos and videos to create games and manipulatives can help children who do not speak your language to have a better understanding of concepts you are teaching.

◆ Make your own electronic games. (Yes, you!) Interactive whiteboards and multitouch tables provide wonderful opportunities for you to create activities and games using your own creativity and expertise. You may even be able to adapt any original games and materials you have already created to work on IWBs and multitouch tables. The developers of these devices have made it fairly simple for teachers to create their own experiences, and you can add new languages whenever you need them (Nemeth & Simon 2012).

◆ Use digital photos to make class books that parents or volunteers can translate into the languages of the children (Nemeth 2009). If you create the book yourself and save it on your computer or device, you can add new languages to it as needed.

◆ Host workshops for parents so they can use your program's technology tools to re-create the toys and games they remember from their childhood. Encourage them to replicate authentic games that reflect their home culture and language.

◆ Download authentic music, rhymes, finger plays, and stories from different countries.

Help DLLs Show What They Know and Can Do

◆ Use digital voice recorders, phones, digital cameras, MP3 players with audio recording, tablets, and smartpens to capture examples of children's speech in their home language and in English (Puerling 2012). Digitally record children acting out stories in their own languages or interacting with peers. Upload the recordings to your computer and include them in children's portfolios.

◆ Look for SMART Table, or other multi-touch tables, and mobile apps that track children's activities. Sophisticated apps are available that collect information on individual children's play to see how far they have progressed in each skill area. The information helps you monitor children's progress and plan based on what children are learning. English-only apps and computer activities can provide valuable information about children's interests and their persistence and progress in English. Although not as common, apps and software activities in the children's home languages allow you to track their progress and show what they know in non-English languages. Another solution is an app that allows children to progress from level to level using activities that focus on nonverbal cues, such as the iPhone/iPad app Memory Train, by Pi'ikea Street.

Connect With Language and Culture Supports

◆ Try Skype, a free program that enables people to have video chats anywhere in the world. You might have a Skype conversation with a class in another country, or have a grandmother on a different continent do a cooking demonstration in her home language.

◆ Conduct research on the Internet to find images that are familiar to the children in your class from their previous home. Use those images to start conversations among children from different backgrounds so they can get to know each other. Children will develop a deeper respect for their peers who look, sound, or dress differently than they do if they have opportunities to share about their families and their personal histories.

◆ Use digital storytelling as a way to help all children build their language and literacy skills in their home languages and in others. An added benefit is the ability to email the recorded stories to relatives and friends anywhere in the world to share and discuss in any language. For more guidance on using digital storytelling, look for "Exploring Elephant Seals in New Jersey: Preschoolers Use Collaborative Multimedia Albums," by Victoria B. Fantozzi, in the May 2012 issue of *Young Children* (Fan-

Technology shouldn't replace the great things already happening in your classroom, but it can enhance and improve the teaching and learning experience when used for a specific purpose.

Free Internet Resources for Teaching DLLs

www.colorincolorado.org

www.voicethread.com (free trial)

www.googletranslate.com

www.googleearth.com

www.mamalisa.com

www.nationalgeographic.com

www.storybird.com

www.icdlbooks.org

tozzi 2012) or in *Spotlight on Young Children and Technology* from NAEYC.

Conclusion

Technology gives you access to languages and resources whenever you need them and lets you easily switch languages without buying a roomful of new supplies. Technology makes it easy to connect and share with children and families across language barriers—and across the world. The availability of resources in the home languages of the children is an important factor, but it is not the only factor needed to help DLLs succeed. DLLs need high-quality, developmentally appropriate learning experiences with enhancements in their home languages. Linguistically diverse technology solutions make it possible to add new languages for English-speaking children as well, enabling them to reap the benefits of learning a second language early on.

Using the technology implementation ideas in this article, you should be able to significantly change the learning environment you provide for young DLLs. As technology brings the world to your fingertips, and takes you and the children on journeys far and wide through digital connections, what you learn about other languages and cultures will undoubtedly make you an even better teacher!

References

Fantozzi, V.B. 2012. "Exploring Elephant Seals in New Jersey: Preschoolers Use Collaborative Multimedia Albums." *Young Children* 67 (3): 42–49.

McManis, L.D., & S.B. Gunnewig. 2012. "Finding the Education in Educational Technology with Early Learners." *Young Children* 67 (3): 14–24. www.naeyc.org/yc/article/finding-education-in-educational-technology.

NAEYC & Fred Rogers Center for Early Learning and Children's Media at Saint Vincent College. 2012. "Technology and Interactive Media as Tools in Early Childhood Programs Serving Children from Birth through Age 8." Joint position statement. Washington, DC: NAEYC. www.naeyc.org/files/naeyc/file/positions/PS_technology_WEB2.pdf.

Nemeth, K.N. 2009. *Many Languages, One Classroom: Teaching Dual and English Language Learners*. Beltsville, MD: Gryphon House.

Nemeth, K.N. 2012. *Basics of Supporting Dual Language Learners: An Introduction for Educators of Children from Birth Through Age 8*. Washington, DC: NAEYC.

Nemeth, K.N., & F.S. Simon. 2012. "Designing a Rubric for Preschool Bilingual Apps." www.ecetech.net/blog/dll/designing-a-rubric-for-preschool-bilingual-apps-by-karen-nemeth.

Puerling, B. 2012. *Teaching in the Digital Age: Smart Tools for Age 3 to Grade 3*. St. Paul, MN: Redleaf.

Simon, F.S., & K.N. Nemeth. 2012. *Digital Decisions: Choosing the Right Technology Tools for Early Childhood Education*. Lewisville, NC: Gryphon House.

Daniel R. Meier

Integrating Content and Mechanics in New Language Learners' Writing

How to Play Baseball
By Cristian (age 7, second grade)

I'm going to teach you how to play baseball. The person behind home plate is called the catcher. If the catcher catches the ball 3 times, you're out. The umpire stands behind the catcher. There are 9 players on a team. When you're going to bat, a person throws a ball to you. You try to hit the ball. If you hit the ball, you run the bases. If you don't get a home run, wait until someone else hits the ball and try to get a home run. Now you know how to play baseball.

Writing and literacy development are crucial for the academic and social success of new language learners in the primary grades (Samway 2006; Gregory 2008; Shagoury 2009). Over the last 25 years, several terms have been used to describe the talents and needs of children learning new languages in early childhood settings. The term that I prefer, and which I use in this article, is *new language learners*. It describes children still at an early stage of learning or "lacking fluency in a second or additional language but whose ultimate aim is to become as fluent as possible, that is, able to communicate easily with others

Challenging Common Myths About DLLs

When DLLs are supported in learning two languages, becoming fluent in both of them, they often develop enhanced executive functions that help them do well in school. For example, when compared to monolingual children, DLLs often have better ability to focus on a task and block out distractions. Fully supporting dual language development is beneficial for all children (p. 7).

Daniel R. Meier is professor of elementary education at San Francisco State University. He teaches courses on language development, reading/language arts, narrative inquiry and memoir, and international education. He is the co-editor of *Educational Change in International Early Childhood: Crossing Borders of Reflection* (Routledge 2014).

Adapted, with permission, from Daniel R. Meier, *Teaching Children to Write: Constructing Meaning and Mastering Mechanics* (New York: Teachers College Press, 2011).

Author's Note: I gratefully acknowledge and thank Florence Tse for contributing her thoughts and strategies about dual language learning to this article.

in the language and able positively to identify with both. . . ." (Gregory 2008, 1).

New language learners need specialized support in linking oral and written language as they develop their writing skills. Of crucial importance in this process, and the focus of this article, is the successful integration of content (ideas, feelings, and information) with mechanics (punctuation, syntax, formats, and genres, such as how-to books, fairy tales, personal narratives, and poetry) across the K–3 spectrum (Meier 2011). This is *the* foundational stage for learning to write well for new language learners—mechanics integration provides *developmentally appropriate* and *linguistically accessible* opportunities for writing growth. During these crucial years, new language learners gain accuracy in writing, confidence, motivation, and voice.

Content and Mechanics Integration in Early Writing—What Is It?

Cristian, a young writer whose home language is Spanish, can help us see new ways to integrate written language mechanics and content. Relatively new to writing in English, Cristian juggles mechanics and content as he composes his how-to book about playing baseball. To create his piece, Cristian benefits from my close scaffolding, the structured format of a how-to piece, and access to his extensive background knowledge about baseball.

As I work with Cristian, I scaffold the integration of specific elements of content and mechanics in his written piece. (See "Promoting Content and Mechanics Integration," p. 75.) I provide help with some spelling and write some sentences he dictates to me. I nudge him along with content questions and prompts. In terms of written language *mechanics*, Cristian carefully sounds out the words as he tries to spell as many words as he can, varies his sentences as he writes and dictates to me, and works hard to make his handwriting legible. He adds varied verb tenses, uses contractions ("I'm" and "you're"), and repeats certain words ("If you hit the ball . . ." and "If you don't get a home run . . .") for alliterative effect.

In terms of written language *content*, Cristian has a wonderful opening line to hook the reader ("I'm going to teach you how to play baseball") and excellent information about baseball as he explains key positions ("The person behind the plate is called the catcher") and logistics ("If you hit the ball, you run the bases"). He explains the rules as he understands them ("If the catcher catches the ball 3 times, you're out"), includes the reader/audience, and anticipates possible scenarios ("If you don't get a home run, wait until someone else hits the ball and try to get a home run"). Cristian shows a masterful understanding of the format or genre of a how-to piece of informational writing.

Written Language Conventions

How do Cristian and other young new language learners benefit from integrating content and mechanics in their writing? The early years of formal schooling are a crucial period for inculcating lifelong habits of and dispositions for writing, and for children to learn sophisticated ways to create powerful, engaging, and masterful writing. Many new language learners become hesitant and reluctant writers in these years. They think they have nothing interesting to write or they feel they don't know how to write.

Children need to master written language conventions to write well, with accuracy and inventiveness. When children gain control over a range of written language conventions across varied writing tasks, they feel a sense of achievement and personal triumph. Most young new language learners gather the momentum and motivation to write something of interest to themselves and others when they believe they have a certain critical mass of knowledge of and control over selected written language conventions. For example, Cristian benefited from my assistance in helping him to gather enough elements of content and mechanics to write his informative and well-written how-to piece on playing baseball. (See "Challenges in Written Language Mechanics" and "Challenges in Written Language Content and Meaning.")

Over time, with direct and indirect guidance, young writers learn to use an expanding repertoire of ways to integrate and connect content and mechanics in their writing.

New Language Learners and Writing—Key Curricular and Instructional Foundations

New language learners are too often portrayed as not fully capable of rich and sophisticated content and mechanics integration in their early writing development (Samway 2006). First, these children are often seen as needing a requisite level of oral language comprehension and production *before* they are ready to learn how to write. But it is precisely this combination of oral language and writing that new language learners need, as oral and written language reinforce and enrich each other.

Second, too often teachers give new language learners only low-level writing activities, such as fill-in-the-blank worksheets, or use only controlled, simple vocabulary that does not motivate children to build cumulative language chunks of the new target language (Gregory 2008). Katharine Samway (2006) notes that young writers learning English are "capable of expressing complex thoughts, even if they do not have control of the English writing system" (30), and can "understand more than they are able to express in writing" (34).

Challenges in Written Language Mechanics

Depending on the target language, new language learners (who are in the beginning stages of learning the basics of syntax, phonology, and orthography in a new language) face the following challenges in terms of written language mechanics (Meier 2011):

- Mastering the physical formation of writing alphabetic letters and characters
- Learning new word meanings and syntactical structures more commonly found in written academic and literary language than daily oral language
- Transferring pauses and stops in oral speech to pauses and stops in written language
- Gaining increasing accuracy in word spellings
- Learning to talk about writing and interact with peers and teachers in socioculturally expected ways

Challenges in Written Language Content and Meaning

New language learners, in the early stages of mastering the vocabulary and text genres in a new language, face the following challenges in terms of written language content and meaning (Meier 2011):

- Garnering the motivation to write something of value and importance in a new language
- Feeling confident enough to make mistakes and seek support from peers and adults
- Understanding various writing genres and formats
- Developing a sense of voice as a writer and as an individual
- Learning to rely on personal background knowledge *and* school-based academic learning

Third, writing instruction for new language learners is too often divorced from other language and symbolic activities, such as art and drama, which can act as developmentally appropriate springboards for language growth.

There are key elements for incorporating successful content/mechanics integration in our writing curriculum and teaching. We can mix and match these elements to fit the specific needs of new language learners. Here are highlights of three elements at the kindergarten level.

Kindergarten—Laying the Foundation for Content/Mechanics Integration

Florence Tse, an English/Chinese bilingual speaker, has taught many first-generation Chinese American children and currently teaches a kindergarten classroom of mostly new language learners from a variety of linguistic backgrounds. Florence ensures new language learners get off to a good start in their content/mechanics integration by using three strategies:

- ◆ Linking drawing and dictation/writing
- ◆ Emphasizing content first, then gradually introducing mechanics elements
- ◆ Using sentence frames and read-alouds of predictable books

Interactive Drawings

Florence starts the school year with interactive drawings rather than direct writing activities. This way the children's earliest writing experiences are not heavily dependent on English oral language proficiency in syntax, phonology, and vocabulary.

> We talk a lot about how to look at our classmates and observe carefully and draw rather than write. For example, if we are drawing portraits of each other, the idea is to look at our friends closely. I model and we draw the pictures together. Then we add writing. We clap how many words they want to use in their sentence to express their thought, and whatever words they do know how to write, we write, and whatever words they don't, they just leave a blank. So there's really no pressure to spell out those words.

Florence plans the writing curriculum to emphasize the power of pictures and drawings as a form of writing (Vygotsky 1978, [1934] 1986; Baghban 2007; Horn & Giacobbe 2007). This provides a predictable format and guided linguistic support for new language learners (Reyes 1992; Samway 2006). For instance, to children unfamiliar with a language the steady stream of oral language often sounds like noise. Florence breaks this down to a target language by clapping, in a one-to-one correspondence, the number of words the children want to use.

> The children in my class begin their drawing journey with explicit lessons on how to draw people with facial features, body features, and clothing. Our drawing lessons help the children pay attention to the setting of their drawings, which helps them attend to the small visual details that help tell their story. Drawings are also valuable forms of symbolic print that do not pressure children to focus only on letters as more abstract symbols. Children acquire new vocabulary through drawing as we teach words for facial features (iris, jaw, nostrils), body features (joints, elbow, hip), and setting (foreground, background, time of day).

Florence also uses the "inside-out approach" (Gregory 2008), which emphasizes small units of language such as letters and sounds. For instance, Florence helps the children clap out the words they want to dictate or write for their sentence. This strategy breaks down English syntax and vocabulary into bite-size chunks and is a developmentally appropriate beginning to writing.

Content First

Florence seeks an overall integration of content and mechanics, but follows a teaching sequence that begins with content.

> I start with content so the children get their ideas out. At the start of the school year, the children are mostly nonverbal in English, so I think it's important that they can state their ideas. So content comes before mechanics— "What's important? What's your point? Why are we writing this?" We always have to be explicit about our writing objectives—we're writing for a purpose.

Although the children have few of the skills needed to produce oral and written English, Florence emphasizes content over mechanics to give their content and ideas a preeminent position as they start their talking/drawing/writing journey. For example, at circle time the children use their drawings and props, such as block people, to act out, talk through, and playfully engage in a process of using symbols and print to tell a story.

As the year progresses, Florence increases attention to mechanics, building on the drawing and story drama content she used earlier.

> I talk about capitalization, spacing between words, correct grammar, and how to figure out if the sentence was about the past, the present, or something happening in the future. I also have the children reread their writing and ask themselves, "Does this make sense?"

By breaking down elements of written conventions, and also paying attention to meaning and content, Florence integrates content and mechanics over the course of the kindergarten year.

Promoting Content and Mechanics Integration

The following elements point to the critical need for increasing our own instructional knowledge of what it means to write well, and how the content/mechanics ratio fits into this overall foundation and set of strategies:

- Deepening our *philosophy* of what it means to write well by emphasizing content/mechanics integration (Moffett 1988)
- Emphasizing *content*, *information*, and *ideas* so new language learners have motivating material to write about (Gregory 2008)
- Expanding our writing *curriculum* so children can experience content/mechanics integration on a daily basis (Calkins 1994; Calkins et al. 2003)
- Basing our instructional strategies for content/mechanics integration on children's *oral language* strengths and talents (Britton 1970)
- Teaching the *writing cycle* or *process* of planning, writing, revising, and sharing (Calkins 1994; Calkins et al. 2003) in developmentally appropriate and culturally responsive ways (Delpit & Dowdy 2008; Copple & Bredekamp 2009)
- Using *prompts* and *frames* for structuring content/mechanics integration (Samway 2006)
- Promoting content/mechanics transfer through *linking reading and writing* activities (Mermelstein 2006)
- Teaching a wide range of written language genres to promote the acquisition of *academic language* (Tabors & Snow 2001)
- Providing daily opportunities for read-alouds of high-quality children's literature (Trelease 2013) and story dictation (Gadzikowski 2007)
- Linking writing with drawing and art and other symbolic exploration (Edwards, Gandini, & Forman 2011)

Sentence Frames and Read-Alouds With Predictable Text

Florence uses developmentally appropriate and linguistically accessible sentence frames, such as, "I like_____" and "The book is about_____," at the beginning of the year. She also plans steps to ensure a "gradual release of responsibility" (Miller 2013, 18) from her modeling and increase the children's composing independence over the course of the year. She emphasizes teacher modeling and chunking language into bite-size pieces, which gives the children a comfortable foundation for early writing. Florence gives direct support and guidance to the children who are mostly nonverbal in English so they can state their ideas in writing.

She employs storybooks and texts with predictable syntactical patterns and engaging content.

> I listen to a lot of the children's conversations during turn-and-talk or at the lunch table. Sometimes their conversations are addressed to me, but sometimes they are shared between friends. They're good jumping-off points for me to see where their writing can go and where they would be most successful. One day we were talking about how we're really in love with books. We had read *I Went Walking,* by Sue Williams, which the children loved. They took the book and made their own sentence frames and made their own books from it.

Florence reads *I Will Never Not Ever Eat a Tomato,* by Lauren Child, as a read-aloud. Afterward, the children discuss their food memories and what they like and don't like to eat. Ming is particularly taken with the book and wants to write about it. She looks at the cover and writes eight blank lines for the words in the title. Then she fills in the blanks for *I* and *a,* which Florence notes are "as much as she could write in English." Ming then brings her paper to Florence, and Florence writes the rest of the title. The structural format of the blank lines and the stress-free activity of copying from a text helped Ming begin to compose.

Florence gradually extends the sentence frames to incorporate sight words *(the, was, I)* from the children's storybooks. She also writes a sentence on paper for the children to cut out, rearrange into a new sentence, copy in their own writing, and then draw a picture for. Over time, this activity helps the children with vocabulary development, sight-word recognition, letter formation, spelling, and linking text with picture.

In November, Florence reads a question with the children. They discuss possible answers, and the children draw pictures to respond to the question. By January, the children draw and write their own responses to Florence's question. Florence circulates around the room as children draw, helping them find a starting point for their written responses. She also encourages children to use peer support to spell out words, especially if they know that a friend can help them sound out a word better than they can alone. Some children have "sentence sense" about the syntactical structures in English they wish to compose, and Florence encourages these children to continue composing while she supports others who need more help with English syntax and spelling. Although the class is not an official Chinese/English bilingual class, Florence readily uses her Cantonese to help the Cantonese-speaking children understand a particular word or phrase.

> I want their ideas to be fluid, to flow, and so sometimes I translate their ideas from Cantonese to English. A child describes his picture in Cantonese to me, and I help him with the words. I say, "These are the words for it in English."

Florence creates her writing curriculum to maximize the children's knowledge of basic functions of languages in general—to inform, entertain, persuade, include, spark thinking, and promote understanding. The children follow a developmentally and linguistically appropriate journey toward a greater integration of written language content and mechanics.

Conclusion

Young new language learners' writing thrives on a healthy daily mix of expert teacher knowledge and guidance, rich oral language, stories and children's literature, dictation, art and drawing, interactions with peers, and engagement with developmentally appropriate elements of the writing process. While we have increasing theoretical and practical knowledge of these elements as discrete parts of effective writing instruction for new language learners, we still need ways to unite these elements in a coherent and cohesive writing curriculum and way of teaching. Focusing on the integration of written language mechanics and content helps us achieve this goal.

The power in children's writing comes bit by bit, over time, as elements of mechanics are integrated with elements of meaning. I recently heard the composer Stephen Sondheim, at 80, reflect on his long career writing musicals. When asked about his process for writing his lyrics and his music, Sondheim explained that he does not compose musicals by first writing the music, and then the lyrics, or vice versa. Rather, he writes a little music, and then adds some lyrics, then a little more music and then more lyrics, and so on until he creates an entire musical.

This is a helpful process to remember—writing for new language learners is essentially an artful dance and continual integration and fusion of content and mechanics. This process is particularly challenging (though ultimately rewarding when they become biliterate) for new language learners. They need our expert support and guidance in learning how to spell, understand word order, and express ideas in new languages.

Writing during the earliest school years is an essential part of a successful education for new language learners. Our challenge and joy during the primary years is to nurture content and mechanics integration as the foundation for successful and rewarding writing throughout life for new language learners. Writing empowers the soul, informs the mind, changes society and human action, and creates memories and ideas and images of great internal and external beauty and perfection. And well-told stories, provocative opinion pieces, poignant letters, informative how-to pieces about baseball, and passionate poetry—all feature a well-balanced mix of content and mechanics that give shape and substance and power to the written word.

Engaging Families

Gina is almost 4 years old, and today is her first day in our preschool program. At home Gina speaks some Spanish with her grandparents and mostly English with her mother. Her mother, Sylvia, learned some Spanish from her parents, but she does not know how to write it. "As a child, my parents sent me to English-only schools and as a result my Spanish is rather limited," Sylvia told us. "My parents thought that learning Spanish would have a negative effect on my ability to learn English. In my current job it'd be an asset if I could speak and write Spanish fluently. I want Gina's experiences to be different from mine. I would like her to be totally fluent in both languages and to be able to read, write, speak, and understand both Spanish and English."

As teachers we have the challenge and the responsibility of finding creative strategies to support Gina and other children in learning English while preserving their family's home languages. To achieve this we plan activities that promote inclusion and collaboration among English-speaking children and children who are learning a second language. We also balance large group activities with small group activities and one-to-one interactions with children who benefit from individual attention. When we do this, we convey to Gina and the other children that we value their home languages and cultures. With the right home and school supports, these children will develop a strong foundation for proficiency in both languages.

—Isauro Michael Escamilla, MA, preschool teacher and university guest lecturer

References

Baghban, M. 2007. "Scribbles, Labels, and Stories: The Role of Drawing in the Development of Writing." *Young Children* 62 (1): 20–26.

Britton, J. 1970. "The Student's Writing." In *Explorations in Children's Writing*, ed. E.L. Evertts, 21-76. Urbana, IL: National Council of Teachers of English.

Calkins, L.M. 1994. *The Art of Teaching Writing*. 2nd ed. Portsmouth, NH: Heinemann.

Calkins, L.M., P. Bleichman, A. Hartman, N. Louis, L. Mermelstein, S. Parsons, L. Pessah, & A.O. Smith. 2003. *Units of Study for Primary Writing: A Yearlong Curriculum*. The Units of Study for Primary Writing: Yearlong Curriculum Series. Portsmouth, NH: Heinemann.

Cooper, P.M. 2009. *The Classrooms All Young Children Need: Lessons in Teaching From Vivian Paley*. Chicago: University of Chicago Press.

Copple, C., & S. Bredekamp, eds. 2009. *Developmentally Appropriate Practice in Early Childhood Programs Serving Children From Birth through Age 8*. Washington, DC: NAEYC.

Delpit, L., & J.K. Dowdy, eds. 2008. *The Skin That We Speak: Thoughts on Language and Culture in the Classroom*. 5th ed. New York: New Press

Edwards, C., L. Gandini, & G. Forman, eds. 2011. *The Hundred Languages of Children: The Reggio Emilia Experience in Transformation*. 3rd ed. Santa Barbara, CA: Praeger.

Fromkin, V., R. Rodman, & N. Hyams. 2013. *An Introduction to Language*. Boston, MA: Cengage.

Gadzikowski, A. 2007. *Story Dictation: A Guide for Early Childhood Professionals*. Minneapolis, MN: Redleaf.

Gregory, E. 2008. *Learning to Read in a New Language*. 2nd ed. London: Sage.

Horn, M., & M.E. Giacobbe. 2007. *Talking, Drawing, Writing: Lessons for Our Youngest Writers*. Portland, ME: Stenhouse.

Meier, D.R. 2011. *Teaching Children to Write: Constructing Meaning and Mastering Mechanics*. New York: Teachers College Press; Berkeley, CA: National Writing Project.

Mermelstein, L. 2006. *Reading/Writing Connections in the K–2 Classroom: Find the Clarity and Then Blur the Lines*. New York: Pearson.

Miller, D. 2002. *Reading With Meaning: Teaching Comprehension in the Primary Grades*. Portland, ME: Stenhouse.

Moffett, J. 1988. *Coming on Center: Essays in English Education*. 2nd ed. Portsmouth, NH: Heinemann.

Neuman, S.B., & T.S. Wright. 2014. "The Magic of Words: Teaching Vocabulary in the Early Childhood Classroom." *The American Educator* 38 (2): 4–13. www.aft.org/pdfs/americaneducator/summer2014/Neuman.pdf.

Reyes, M. de la Luz. 1992. "Challenging Venerable Assumptions: Literacy Instruction for Linguistically Different Students." *Harvard Educational Review* 62 (4): 427–46.

Samway, K.D. 2006. *When English Language Learners Write: Connecting Research to Practice, K–8*. Portsmouth, NH: Heinemann.

Shagoury, R. 2009. "Language to Language: Nurturing Writing Development in Multilingual Classrooms." *Young Children* 64 (2): 52–57.

Tabors, P.O., & C. Snow, 2001. "Young Bilingual Children and Early Literacy Development." *Handbook of Early Literacy Research*, eds. S.B. Neuman & D.K. Dickinson, 159–78. New York: Guilford.

Trelease, J. 2013. *The Read-Aloud Handbook*. 7th ed. New York: Viking Penguin.

Vygotsky, L.S. [1934] 1986. *Thought and Language*. Cambridge, MA: MIT Press.

Vygotsky, L.S. 1978. *Mind in Society: The Development of Higher Psychological Processes*. Cambridge, MA: Harvard University Press.

Paula Moujalli,
Laura Haim,
Ryan W. Pontier

naeyc® 2, 3, 10

Principles for Leading a Dual Language Program

Three-year-old Joan (pronounced *Jon*) sits in the art area surrounded by buttons, yarn, small colored sticks, and other collage materials. As part of their investigation of faces, Joan and his classmates have been paying attention to ways facial expressions can communicate feelings. Ms. Adriana just read the book *Así me siento (This Is the Way I Feel),* and now Joan is moving around the materials to represent different feelings. As he places a stick straight across the face to represent his mouth, he looks up at Ms. Adriana and says, "Así es cuando estoy triste *(this is how it is when I'm sad).* And when I'm happy, I smile." Ms. Adriana replies, "Tú cambiaste la boca para expresar las emociones *(you changed the mouth to express emotions)."*

At first, you might think that Joan confuses his languages or that he cannot keep track of which language to use. However, Joan, an emergent bilingual whose family immigrated to the United States from Peru, is employing a practical way of communicating called *code switching* (García and Kleifgen 2010). Code switching involves using multiple languages to make sense of the world and to be understood when communicating with others (Genesee 2009). It enables Joan to express himself in two languages.

Joan attends the United Way Center for Excellence in Early Education Demonstration School, Educare of Miami-Dade.

Paula Moujalli, MEd, is the director/principal of the United Way Center for Excellence in Early Education Demonstration School, Educare of Miami-Dade. She was born and raised in Venezuela and has two sons who attended a dual language program.

Laura Haim, MEd, leads professional learning at the United Way Center for Excellence in Early Education. She began her career teaching in a dual language kindergarten class as a Teach for America corps member in Phoenix.

Ryan W. Pontier, PhD, is a professor of bilingualism and biliteracy in the early childhood education program in the School of Education at Miami Dade College. He also began his career as a Teach for America corps member and has taught in two dual language schools, one in Texas and one in Miami. He earned his doctorate in language and literacy learning in multilingual settings.

The center is an innovative learning, teaching, and training initiative dedicated to elevating the quality of early care and education. It models proven best practices through its demonstration school and, through its professional learning programs, shares those practices with adult learners, including families, educators, and early care and education providers.

The demonstration school is a dual language program serving infants through preschoolers. The program

- Uses research-based practices to support children's learning in both English and Spanish, enabling children to acquire fluency and early literacy skills in both languages
- Supports children as they experience the rewards and challenges associated with learning two languages
- Embraces the linguistic and cultural diversity of children and families

In addition to large group experiences in Spanish and English, each classroom has one teacher who serves as the English language model and one teacher who serves as the Spanish language model to facilitate the use of both languages throughout the day. In this environment, Joan and his peers work toward becoming bilinguals, learning to use both languages to differing degrees and for a variety of purposes.

Leadership is critical to the program's success since leaders establish the environment in which multiple languages are not only supported but also celebrated. In this article, we explain the benefits of a dual language program for children and families and describe a series of guiding principles for administrators or directors who are considering implementing a dual language program. These principles are supported by research and our program practices.

Why a Dual Language Program?

A dual language program offers children an authentic and meaningful context in which to learn two languages (Lindholm-Leary 2001). This in turn results in many short-term and long-term benefits. Knowing another language can increase children's self-esteem and self-confidence because it helps them feel more at ease and creates a natural flexibility and adaptability. When children learn two languages, they gain a wider cultural experience, including multiple ways of understanding and interpreting the world. Children who know more than one language show greater creativity and problem-solving skills in verbal and math problems (Baker 2014). Children who are strong speakers in their first language tend to have stronger literacy skills in their second language and more easily acquire additional languages later on (Tabors 2008). As with everything we do, by supporting children's bilingualism, we are preparing children for school and life. Given the rapidly globalizing economy, children who speak two or more languages will find more job opportunities available to them as adults.

A program that nurtures and celebrates language is an inviting place for families. Families feel comfortable when they can communicate with their children's teachers and when they know those professionals will nurture their children's ability to communicate using two languages.

More than half the people in Miami-Dade County were born in another country, and 72 percent of residents speak a language other than English at home (U.S. Census Bureau 2014). To date, families who join our program speak English, Spanish, or a combination of the two, and many speak additional languages as well. Spanish-speaking families appreciate the fact that because our program supports both English and Spanish, their children will not lose their home languages or the connections that home languages provide to culture and family (Fillmore 1991).

Implementing a Dual Language Program

Dual language programs may take a variety of approaches, but our experiences and research have led us to follow the principles discussed here.

Yo no traduzco; yo hablo español. Apoyada por el ambiente que les rodea y las experiencias que les proveemos en ambos lenguajes, los niños se van familiarizando con ambos idiomas. Valoro el poder fomentar y desarrollar en los niños el amor por el español que está en ocasiones ligado a sus raíces culturales. De igual manera, como hispanoparlante me he beneficiado del programa bilingüe ya que luego de llegar de mi país de origen hace casi cuatro años siento que diariamente mejoro mi inglés.

I do not translate; I speak Spanish. Supported by the environment that surrounds them and the experiences we provide them linguistically, the children have familiarized themselves with both languages. I appreciate the power to encourage and develop in children a love for the Spanish language, a language that for many is linked to their cultural roots. Similarly, as a Spanish speaker I have benefited from the bilingual program. Since arriving from my country of origin almost four years ago, I feel that I have been able to greatly improve my English.

—Adriana, teacher

Understand each child's stage of linguistic development and respond with appropriate support. Children who enter our program as infants or toddlers learn two languages simultaneously. They are developing the concepts of language and communication across the two languages. Although they are learning two languages, they follow the same linguistic stages as children who are learning only one language, and they experience these milestones at the same time as monolingual infants and toddlers (De Houwer 2009). The children cry, coo, babble, use one word and then two words, and finally use expanded statements.

It is important for early childhood education teachers and other caregivers to take into account what the child is doing in *all* of her languages. For example, 2-year-old Anna finishes her cereal and tells Ms. Veronica, "I want *más*." Anna is producing a whole sentence, and like Joan, she includes some English and some Spanish. If teachers are unaware of the English or Spanish elements and what they mean, they may not recognize this as a complete sentence.

Monolingual children who enter our program as preschoolers acquire a second language sequentially. They experience the typical stages of second language acquisition: first language use, observation of the use of the second language, telegraphic *(Mommy up!)* and formulaic (frequently using *I want . . .* and finishing the phrase appropriately) language use in the second language, and productive language (Tabors 2008). The observation stage should not be misconstrued as a developmental or language delay since it is typical for monolingual preschoolers to experience a quiet phase during which they are attending to others' use of the second language.

Regardless of whether a child experiences simultaneous or sequential bilingualism, it is important to consider *all* of a child's linguistic development, not only what she can do

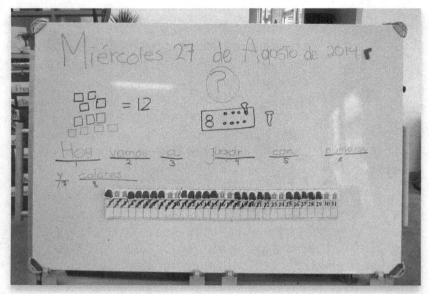

in one language.

Plan for intentional instruction and authentic experiences in each language. In each classroom the English language model and the Spanish language model teachers maintain their respective languages at all times. The teachers alternate weekly leading the large group activities and experiences. For example, over the course of one week, the lesson plan, the message of the day, morning circle, the focal books used for read-alouds, and instructions for other large group activities are delivered entirely in Spanish. During this week, the English language model teacher interacts with children in English when appropriate (for example, to ask appropriate questions, clarify statements from children and the other teacher, address challenging behavior), but the Spanish language model teacher takes the lead. The two teachers then switch roles the following week.

Although there are always two languages used in the classroom, simultaneous translation (saying something in one language and immediately translating it to another *throughout the course of the lesson*) is discouraged by teachers, administrators, and policy makers since it often causes learners to tune out the new language and wait for the translation in the language with which they are comfortable (Baker 2014). Our structure provides authentic, meaningful experiences for children in each language. We have found that at the beginning of the school year, monolingual preschool children often seek out the teacher who speaks their home language. As they spend more time with their teachers, however, they begin to approach both teachers in their respective languages. For example, in March, preschooler Emilio commented to his mom, "I speak Spanish with Adriana. I don't speak English with her."

The intentional use of language by teachers extends to printed materials as well. All text, including fliers and documentation panels, is presented to children and families in both languages. English text is in black and Spanish text is in blue so the children begin to differentiate them.

Accept children's responses regardless of what language(s) they choose to use. Both Spanish and English are used throughout the day. There is no designated time in which children can speak only Spanish or only English. Rather, they comfortably express themselves in English, Spanish, or a combination of the two.

Collect formal and informal evidence of children's development. A standardized assessment is a snapshot in time and may not accurately reflect a child's language proficiency, content knowledge, and skills, especially if an assessment is administered in only one language. When possible, we gather a variety of data about children's skills in all of their languages. We explain to families whose children are sequential bilinguals that children's scores on standardized assessments, such as kindergarten readiness exams, may be lower when taken in the second language; this is to be expected since they are just beginning to learn a new language. We remind them that such exams are therefore not an accurate reflection of their children's overall knowledge and skills. We also regularly use language assessments to chart children's bilingual and biliterate development.

Welcome families by using both languages. We tell families that we value their languages in a myriad of ways—from communicating with them in their preferred language to inviting them to share their culture during Week of the Young Child classroom events. All printed and verbal communications are in both English and Spanish, and we plan family events and meetings in both languages so that everyone understands the content. At times we translate for parents in the moment. All developmental screenings conducted in collaboration with families are completed in English and Spanish so they are accurate.

Strengthen the connection between school and home. We educate families on the program's dual language approach and the value of using more than one language with children. This begins at the before-school orientation and continues while the child is part of the program. We often create workshops and monthly roundtables at the center where families suggest topics of interest and have an opportunity to interact with each other and an expert on the topic. This offers families the opportunity to share ideas and concerns in their home language.

Learning a second language can be daunting for some monolingual families, so we offer resources and guidance to help them encourage their children as they acquire a new language. Families often ask us to translate words their children are using at home. For example, a parent who speaks English and German to her child asked the teacher to define the Spanish words her child had been using at home—*agua*, *sopa*, *jabón*, *leche*, and *vamos*. The teacher proudly provided verbal and written translations so that the mother could continue to support her child's trilingual development. We also provide resources for families to support their child's language acquisition.

Recognize cultural diversity, even among speakers of the same language. It is important to learn from all families and respect their individual cultures. The program includes children from more than 12 Spanish-speaking countries, all with their own cultures. We understand that although the language is shared, there is great diversity among families' home countries and experiences. Staff work hard to understand and acknowledge that Spanish has many varieties. For example, families may speak different dialects of Spanish depending on what country—and even what *part* of the country—they are from. This is evidenced in language choice: Cuban-American families may say *bananas*, Venezuelan families may say *cambor*, and Spanish families might call them *plátanos*.

Engage families. A map posted at the entrance of the center shows where families are from to increase awareness of our diverse population. An annual potluck dinner features food from different countries. Since we use the project approach, we invite family members and community members to visit the school and talk with the children about their areas of expertise, their cultural practices, their ways of using language, and their styles of interacting. One father who is an architect showed the children his process for designing buildings. We also pass a journal back and forth between each family and the teacher—written in English and Spanish. Finally, advertising our open door policy lets families know they are always welcome, and each child's primary teacher conducts home visits twice a year and holds monthly conferences to learn about each family.

Attracting and Supporting High-Quality Teachers

The center attracts high-quality, diverse teachers who add depth to our staff because we give them the opportunity to teach in their home language(s). We recruit and hire teachers from the countries represented in our community. Sixty-nine percent of the early childhood workforce in Miami-Dade County identifies Spanish as their primary language (Clements, Kalifeh, & Grass 2014). Teachers are drawn to our program because of the opportunity to advance their professional development and possibly learn another language. The teachers are exposed to the other language the same way the children are, so they begin a similar process of language acquisition.

Select teachers who are comfortable in the dual language setting. We need teachers who are proficient in English or Spanish. During the hiring process we explain to candidates our dual language program and what that means in terms of instruction, and then we ask how comfortable they would be in this environment. It's not mandatory to speak both languages, but it is preferred. We ensure they are proficient in the language—candidates must read, write, and speak the language well. It is important for prospective teachers to understand both our approach and the goal of providing children with authentic experiences in two languages. We look for people who can maintain their assigned language and communicate the value of this experience to families. In addition, we present scenarios and ask questions

Being a monolingual in a dual language environment has proven to be a learning experience for me. Communication is fundamental as an educator: communication with the children, families, and colleagues. At the beginning, and to this day, body language plays a large role when I am interpreting and communicating with Spanish speakers. As I adjusted to the dual language environment, I started to pick up the language and I understood more. I felt more comfortable connecting and developing relationships with children and parents.

—Heidi, teacher

related to cultural and linguistic diversity to gauge candidates' sensitivity to families' needs. We also have a bilingual floater who can fill in when a teacher is absent.

Provide opportunities to create shared meaning among teachers. We continually support teachers through a variety of professional learning experiences. Based on each teacher's background, we establish an action plan for her to increase her knowledge about language and culture. We refer teachers to workshops and webinars and have open conversations about what they've learned.

We also facilitate reflective practice groups that meet weekly during nap time in which we present situations and discuss how best to use each language. Recently Ms. Columba was reading aloud a story in Spanish, and she made a comment about the character's dress: "Este vestido es tan *fancy*." Like Joan, the teacher code switched because there is no exact word for "fancy" in Spanish—*elegante*, *formal*, and *fino* come close, but all have slightly different connotations. The teacher brought this experience to her reflective practice group. The teachers' animated discussion on the topic honed their awareness of the power of language.

These practice groups foster discussion on language and shared decision making about translations while allowing recognition of individual differences that may arise from teachers' or children's backgrounds.

Conclusion

There are many myths about dual language acquisition, including the incorrect assumption that learning two languages in childhood can result in language delays. Guided by the principles described above, administrators and directors of dual language programs can implement a program that offers numerous benefits for children, families, and teachers.

Engaging Families

When we enroll a child who does not speak English and whose home language is not spoken by our staff, our team brainstorms strategies for welcoming the child and family to the center. We learn a few words in the child's home language to use on the first day. We encourage the family to share their concerns, viewing them as experts on their child.

One class includes a child who speaks Arabic; during the child's first days in the classroom the teacher used the Google translator on her computer to communicate with him. One day she typed "Mom is coming later." As the child heard the translation from the computer, he smiled at the teacher and said, "Okay." After a couple of weeks in the program, this child used body language to communicate and socialized more. While he spoke Arabic in the classroom, he also began to repeat English words he heard from others. In situations like this one we meet more frequently with the family so we can collaborate and better understand what they may need from us.

As an administrator I have learned the importance of openly communicating with families, learning about their cultures, and supporting them at all times. I have also learned that not all strategies work with each dual language learner, so we try one thing at a time until we see what works. We appreciate and support the families' interactions with their children and with us, and we try to learn as much as we can from them. We continually search for an understanding of what we need to do as a dual language program.

—Paula Moujalli

Considerations for Troubleshooting

When designing a dual language program, consider the following questions:

- What are your program's goals?
- What is the program's language philosophy?
- What is the approach to instruction?
- What opportunities exist for families to be engaged in the program?
- How do teachers create shared meaning?
- How do teachers assess children's development?

References

Baker, C. 2014. *A Parents' and Teachers' Guide to Bilingualism*. 4th ed. Clevedon, UK: Multilingual Matters.

Clements, M., P. Kalifeh, & S. Grass. 2014. *Miami-Dade Quality Counts Workforce Study: Early Care and Education Research to Practice Brief*. Tallahassee, FL: The Children's Forum. www.fcforum.org/downloads/news/QCCC%20Workforce%20Study.pdf.

De Houwer, A. 2009. *Bilingual First Language Acquisition*. Clevedon, UK: Multilingual Matters.

Fillmore, L.W. 1991. "When Learning a Second Language Means Losing the First." *Early Childhood Research Quarterly* 6 (3): 323–46. http://psych.stanford.edu/~babylab/pdfs/sdarticle.pdf

García, O., & J.A. Kleifgen. 2010. *Educating Emergent Bilinguals: Policies, Programs, and Practices for English Language Learners*. New York: Teachers College Press.

Genesee, F.H. 2009. "Early Childhood Bilingualism: Perils and Possibilities." *Journal of Applied Research on Learning* 2 (2): 1–21. www.ccl-cca.ca/pdfs/JARL/Jarl-Vol2Art2-Genesse_EN.pdf.

Lindholm-Leary, K.J. 2001. *Dual Language Education*. Clevedon, UK: Multilingual Matters.

Tabors, P.O. 2008. *One Child, Two Languages: A Guide for Early Childhood Educators of Children Learning English as a Second Language*, 2nd ed. Baltimore, MD: Brookes.

U.S. Census Bureau. 2014. "State and County Quick Facts, Miami-Dade County, Florida." Revised July 8. http://quickfacts.census.gov/qfd/states/12/12086.html.

Resources for Supporting Dual Language Learners

NAEYC Resources

Akcan, S. 2014. "Connecting Grammar to Meaning for Children Learning English as a Foreign Language." *Young Children* 69 (3): 22–27.

Amaro-Jiménez, C. 2014. "Lessons Learned From a Teacher Working With Culturally and Linguistically Diverse Children." *Young Children* 69 (1): 32–37.

Axelrod, Y. 2014. "'Todos Vamos a Jugar, Even the Teachers'—Everyone Playing Together." *Young Children* 69 (2): 24–31.

Brereton, A. E. 2010. "Is Teaching Sign Language in Early Childhood Classrooms Feasible for Busy Teachers and Beneficial for Children?" *Young Children* 65 (4): 92–97.

Cheatham, G.A., & Y.E. Ro. 2010. "Young English Learners' Interlanguage as a Context for Language and Early Literacy Development." *Young Children* 65 (4): 18–23.

Cheatham, G.A., & R.M. Santos. 2011. "Collaborating With Families From Diverse Cultural and Linguistic Backgrounds: Considering Time and Communication Orientations." *Young Children* 66 (5): 76–82.

Chen, J.J., & S.H. Shire. 2011. "Strategic Teaching: Fostering Communication Skills in Diverse Young Learners." *Young Children* 66 (2): 20–27.

Chu, M. 2014. "Preparing Tomorrow's Early Childhood Educators: Observe and Reflect About Culturally Responsive Teachers." *Young Children* 69 (2): 82–87.

DeBey, M., & D. Bombard. 2007. "Expanding Children's Boundaries: An Approach to Second-Language Learning and Cultural Understanding." *Young Children* 62 (2): 88–93.

Epstein, A. 2014. *The Intentional Teacher: Choosing the Best Strategies for Young Children's Learning.* Rev. ed. Washington, DC: NAEYC; Ypsilanti, MI: HighScope Educational Research Foundation.

Espinosa, L. 2010. *Getting It Right for Young Children From Diverse Backgrounds: Applying Research to Improve Practice.* Upper Saddle River, NJ: Prentice Hall; Washington, DC: NAEYC.

Genishi, C., & A.H. Dyson. 2009. *Children, Language, and Literacy: Diverse Learners in Diverse Times.* New York: Teacher College Press; Washington, DC: NAEYC.

Gillanders, C., & D.C. Castro. 2011. "Storybook Reading for Young Dual Language Learners." *Young Children* 66 (1): 91–95. www.naeyc.org/files/yc/file/201101/GillandersR_Online0111.pdf.

Klefstad, J.M., & K.C. Martinez. 2013. "Promoting Young Children's Cultural Awareness and Appreciation Through Multicultural Books." *Young Children* 68 (5): 74–81.

Koralek, D., & A. Shillady. 2012. *NEXT for Young Children: An NAEYC Professional Development Resource.* Special Edition No. 1.

Macrina, M., D. Hoover, & C. Becker. 2009. "The Challenge of Working With Dual Language Learners. Three Perspectives: Supervisor, Mentor, and Teacher." *Young Children* 64 (2): 27–34.

NAEYC. 1995. *Responding to Linguistic and Cultural Diversity: Recommendations for Effective Early Childhood Education.* Position statement. Washington, DC: NAEYC. www.naeyc.org/positionstatements/linguistic.

NAEYC. 2013. "Supporting Dual Language Learners and Their Families." Cluster theme. *Young Children* 68 (1). www.naeyc.org/yc/pastissues/2013/march.

NAEYC. 2104. "About the Engaging Diverse Families Project." Accessed August 4. www.naeyc.org/familyengagement/about.

Nemeth, K.N. 2009. "Meeting the Home Language Mandate: Practical Strategies for All Classrooms." *Young Children* 64 (2): 36–42.

Nemeth, K.N. 2012. *Basics of Supporting Dual Language Learners: An Introduction for Educators of Children From Birth Through Age 8.* Washington, DC: NAEYC.

Nemeth. K.N. 2014. "A Guide for Writers on Addressing Linguistic and Cultural Differences." NAEYC. Accessed August 5. www.naeyc.org/files/naeyc/file/NAEYCWritingGuide_CulturalDifferences.pdf.

Patè, M. 2009. "Language and Social Development in a Multilingual Classroom: A Dinosaur Project Enriched With Block Play." *Young Children* 64 (4): 12–19.

Special thanks to Karen N. Nemeth for her contributions to this resource list.

Pilonieta, P., P.L. Shue, & B.T. Kissle. 2014 "Reading Books, Writing Books: Reading and Writing Come Together in a Dual Language Classroom." *Young Children* 69 (3): 14–21.

Shagoury, R. 2009. "Language to Language: Nurturing Writing Development in Multilingual Classrooms." In *Spotlight on Young Children: Exploring Language and Literacy,* ed. A. Shillady, 51–56. Washington, DC: NAEYC.

Souto-Manning, M. 2013. "Research in Review: Teaching Young Children From Immigrant and Diverse Families." *Young Children* 68 (4): 72–79.

Wessels, S., & G. Trainin. 2014. "Bringing Literacy Home: Latino Families Supporting Children's Literacy Learning." *Young Children* 69 (3): 40–46.

Other Articles, Books, and Additional Resources

Barnett, W.S., D.J. Yarosz, J. Thomas, K. Jung, & D. Blanco. 2007. "Two-Way and Monolingual Immersion in Preschool Education: An Experimental Comparison." *Early Childhood Research Quarterly* 22 (3): 277–93.

Barrueco, S., M. Lopez, C. Ong, & P. Lozano. 2012. *Assessing Spanish–English Bilingual Preschoolers: A Guide to Best Approaches and Measures.* Baltimore, MD: Brookes.

Beaty, J. J., & L. Pratt. 2011. *Early Literacy in Preschool and Kindergarten: A Multicultural Perspective.* 3rd ed. Boston, MA: Pearson Allyn & Bacon.

Bialystok, E., & M.M. Martin. 2004. "Attention and Inhibition in Bilingual Children: Evidence From the Dimensional Change Card Sort Task." *Developmental Science* 7 (3): 325–39.

Castro, D.C., L.M. Espinosa, & M.M. Páez. 2011. "Defining and Measuring Quality in Early Childhood Practices That Promote Dual Language Learners' Development and Learning." In *Quality Measurement in Early Childhood Settings,* eds. M. Zaslow, I. Martinez-Beck, K. Tout, & T. Halle, 257–80. Baltimore, MD: Brookes.

Castro, D.C., C. Gillanders, M.B. Machado-Casas, & V. Buysse. 2006. *Nuestros Niños Early Language and Literacy Program.* Chapel Hill: University of North Carolina, Frank Porter Graham Child Development Institute.

Collins, M.F. 2010. "ELL Preschools' English Vocabulary Acquisition From Storybook Reading." *Early Childhood Research Quarterly* 25 (1): 84–97.

Council for Exceptional Children Division for Early Childhood (DEC). 2010. "Responsiveness to ALL Children, Families, and Professionals: Integrating Cultural and Linguistic Diversity Into Policy and Practice." Position statement. Missoula, MT: DEC. http://dec.membershipsoftware.org/files/Position%20State ment%20and%20Papers/Position%20Statement_ Cultural%20and%20Linguistic%20Diversity.pdf.

Dennis, K., & T. Azpiri. 2005. *Sign to Learn: American Sign Language in the Early Childhood Classroom.* St. Paul, MN: Redleaf Press.

Dragan, P.B. 2005. *A How-to Guide for Teaching English Language Learners in the Primary Classroom.* Portsmouth, NH: Heinemann. Available from NAEYC.

Dyson, A.H. 2013. *ReWRITING the Basics: Literacy Learning in Children's Cultures.* New York: Teachers College Press.

Espinosa, L.M. 2013. *PreK–3rd: Challenging Common Myths About Dual Language Learners: An Update to the Seminal 2008 Report.* Foundation for Child Development. www.fcd-us.org/sites/default/files/Challeng ing%20Common%20Myths%20Update.pdf.

Fort, P., & R. Stechuk. 2008. "The Cultural Responsiveness and Dual Language Education Project." *The Journal of ZERO TO THREE* 29 (1): 24–28.

García, E.E., & E.H. García. 2012. *Understanding the Language Development and Early Education of Hispanic Children.* New York: Teachers College Press.

Genesee, F. 2008. "Early Dual Language Learning." *The Journal of ZERO TO THREE* 29 (1): 17–23.

Goldenberg, C. 2008. "Teaching English Language Learners: What the Research Does—and Does Not—Say." *American Educator* 32 (2): 8–19, 22–23, 42–44.

Goldstein, B.A., ed. 2012. *Bilingual Language Development and Disorders in Spanish–English Speakers.* 2nd ed. Baltimore, MD: Brookes.

Gonzalez-Mena, J. 2007. *Diversity in Early Care and Education: Honoring Differences.* 5th ed. New York: McGraw Hill.

Governor's State Advisory Council on Early Learning and Care. *California's Best Practices for Preschool Dual Language Learners: Research Overview Papers.* 2013. Sacramento, CA: Department of Education. www.cde. ca.gov/sp/cd/ce/documents/dllresearchpapers.pdf.

Gutiérrez, K.D., M. Zepeda, & D.C. Castro. 2010. "Advancing Early Literacy Learning for All Children: Implications of the NELP Report for Dual-Language Learners." *Educational Researcher* 39 (4): 334–39.

Hammer, C.S., S. Scarpino, & M.D. Davison. 2011. "Beginning With Language: Spanish–English Bilingual Preschoolers' Early Literacy Development." Chap. 8 in *Handbook of Early Literacy Research,* Vol. 3, eds. S.B. Neuman & D.K. Dickinson, 118–35. New York: The Guilford Press.

Han, W-J. 2012. "Bilingualism and Academic Achievement." *Child Development* 83 (1): 300–21.

Herrera, S.G., D.R. Perez, S.K. Kavimandan, & S. Wessels. 2013. *Accelerating Literacy for Diverse Learners: Strategies for the Common Core Classroom, K–8.* New York: Teachers College Press.

Howes, C., J.T. Downer, & R.C. Pianta. 2011. *Dual Language Learners in the Early Childhood Classroom.* Baltimore, MD: Brookes. Available from NAEYC.

Lugo-Neris, M.J., C.W. Jackson, & H. Goldstein. 2010. "Facilitating Vocabulary Acquisition of Young English Language Learners." *Language, Speech & Hearing Services in Schools* 41(3): 314–27.

Matera, C. 2011. "Supporting Early Writing in Dual Language Head Start Classrooms." *NHSA Dialog* 14 (3): 147–50.

National Center on Cultural and Linguistic Responsiveness. 2014. "Dual Language Learners in State Early Learning Guidelines and Standards." Head Start. Last updated September 15. www.eclkc.ohs.acf.hhs.gov/hslc/tta-system/cultural-linguistic/center/state-guidelines/dll_guidelines.html.

National Governors Association (NGA). 2013. *A Governor's Guide to Early Literacy: Getting All Students Reading by Third Grade.* Washington, DC: NGA. www.nga.org/files/live/sites/NGA/files/pdf/2013/1310NGA EarlyLiteracyReportWeb.pdf.

Nemeth, K.N. 2009. *Many Languages, One Classroom: Teaching Dual and English Language Learners.* Silver Spring, MD: Gryphon House. Available from NAEYC.

Nemeth, K.N. 2012. *Many Languages, Building Connections: Supporting Infants and Toddlers Who Are Dual Language Learners.* Silver Spring, MD: Gryphon House. Available from NAEYC.

Nemeth, K.N., ed. 2014. *Young Dual Language Learners: A Guide for PreK–3 Leaders.* Philadelphia: Caslon Publishing.

Nemeth, K. 2015. "Technology to Support Dual Language Learners." Chap. 9 in *Technology and Digital Media in the Early Years: Tools for Teaching and Learning,* ed. C. Donohue. New York: Routledge; Washington, DC: NAEYC.

Páez, M.M., K.P. Bock, & L. Pizzo. 2011. "Supporting the Language and Early Literacy Skills of English Language Learners: Effective Practices and Future Directions." Chap. 9 in *Handbook of Early Literacy Research,* vol. 3, eds. S.B. Neuman & D.K. Dickinson, 136–52. New York: Guilford Press.

Pandey, A. 2012. *Language Building Blocks: Essential Linguistics for Early Childhood Educators.* New York: Teachers College Press.

Paradis, J., F. Genesee, & M.B. Crago. 2011. *Dual Language Development and Disorders: A Handbook on Bilingualism and Second Language Learning.* 2nd ed. Baltimore, MD: Brookes.

Passe, A.S. 2013. *Dual-Language Learners Birth to Grade 3: Strategies for Teaching English.* St. Paul, MN: Redleaf Press.

Pearson, B.Z. 2008. *Raising a Bilingual Child: A Step-By-Step Guide for Parents.* New York: Random House.

Roberts, T.A. 2009. *No Limits to Literacy for Preschool English Learners.* Thousand Oaks, CA: Corwin.

Rosenkoetter, S.E., & J. Knapp-Philo, eds. 2006. *Learning to Read the World: Language and Literacy in the First Three Years.* Washington, DC: ZERO TO THREE.

Samson, J.F., & B.A. Collins. 2012. *Preparing All Teachers to Meet the Needs of English Language Learners: Applying Research to Policy and Practice for Teacher Effectiveness.* Washington, DC: Center for American Progress. http://cdn.americanprogress.org/wp-content/uploads/issues/2012/04/pdf/ell_report.pdf.

Shanahan, T., & C.J. Lonigan. 2013. *Early Childhood Literacy: The National Early Literacy Panel and Beyond.* Baltimore, MD: Brookes.

Slavin, R., N. Madden, M. Calderón, A. Chamberlain, & M. Hennessy. 2011. "Reading and Language Outcomes of a Multiyear Randomized Evaluation of Transitional Bilingual Education." *Educational Evaluation and Policy Analysis* 33 (1): 47–58.

Souto-Manning, M. 2013. *Multicultural Teaching in the Early Childhood Classroom: Approaches, Strategies and Tools, Preschool–2nd Grade.* New York: Teachers College Press; Washington, DC: Association for Childhood Education International.

Tabors, P.O. 2008. *One Child, Two Languages: A Guide for Early Childhood Educators of Children Learning English as a Second Language.* 2nd ed. Baltimore, MD: Brookes.

Teachers of English to Speakers of Other Languages (TESOL). 2010. "Position Paper on Language and Literacy Development for Young English Language Learners (Ages 3–8)." Alexandria, VA: TESOL. www.tesol.org/docs/pdf/371.pdf?sfvrsn=2.

Web Resources

Babies—This documentary takes viewers on a one-year journey of four babies who live in Namibia, Japan, Mongolia, and California. The film shows the babies eating, sleeping, and socializing and gives the audience an opportunity to explore and examine parenting styles in a global context. www.focus features.com/babies

Becoming Bilingual—Actress Rita Moreno hosts this 30-minute PBS program that examines the challenges of teaching children a new language. The show visits six cities across the country to learn how schools are working to create bilingual readers. *Becoming Bilingual* is the seventh episode of the series *Launching Young Readers*. The program can be viewed on the website. www.readingrockets.org/shows/launching/bilingual

Center for Applied Linguistics (CAL)—This organization promotes access and mutual understanding for linguistically and culturally diverse people around the world. The site's resource center provides briefs, reports, resources, databases, and publications. www.cal.org

Center for Early Care and Education Research–Dual Language Learners—The CECER-DLL project reviews and summarizes the available research on early childhood education for DLLs and offers a comprehensive collection of reports, recommendations, and policy briefs. http://www.cecerdll.fpg.unc.edu

¡Colorín Colorado!—This bilingual (Spanish and English) website is for families and educators of dual language learners. It offers webcasts, newsletters, bilingual booklists, and research and reports about dual language learners and effective instruction. Also included are lists of children's books featuring a variety of cultures and heritages, including American Indian/Alaskan Native, Asian Pacific, and African. www.colorincolorado.org

Día: Diversity in Action—Día is an initiative to emphasize the importance of literacy to children from all backgrounds. The website offers resources for librarians, families, and communities to celebrate diversity using the books and materials available to libraries. http://dia.ala.org

Everything ESL—Written by an ESL teacher and author with more than 34 years of experience, this website suggests lesson plans, teaching tips, and resources for teachers. www.everythingesl.net

The International Children's Digital Library—This organization's goal is to build a collection of outstanding children's literature in languages from around the world. Visitors can use the site's search engine to find online books by age group and language. A Teacher Training Manual offers tips for using the search engine and building on book content in the classroom. http://en.childrenslibrary.org

Language Castle—This site provides resources, teaching tips, and a newsletter for early childhood educators working with children birth through age 6 who are dual language learners. www.language castle.com

The Linguistic Genius of Babies—Dr. Patricia Kuhl describes her language development research in this popular TED Talk video. With video clips showing the advanced brain scanning equipment her team uses to detect brain activity during language learning, Dr. Kuhl explains the importance of human social interactions in the development of first and second languages. Subtitles for the video are available in 44 languages. www.ted.com/talks/patricia_kuhl_the_linguistic_genius_of_babies

Mind in the Making: 42 Books and Tips That Promote Life Skills—Mind in the Making and First Book offer a book collection that combines children's books with tips for building the seven essential life skills discussed in *Mind in the Making*. The three book collections are designed for different age categories, and several books are available in Spanish. http://mindinthemaking.org/firstbook/

National Center on Cultural and Linguistic Responsiveness—NCCLR provides the Head Start community and others with research-based resources, practices, and strategies to support diverse children and families. The site includes webcasts, a bilingual glossary, a program checklist, hands-on strategies in Quick Guides for Teachers, and other resources. www.eclkc.ohs.acf.hhs.gov/hslc/tta-system/cultural-linguistic

National Clearinghouse for English Language Acquisition—The NCELA collects and disseminates research and resources that supports high-quality education for English language learners. The website offers a free archive of webinars, professional development resources, and Title III information and resources. www.ncela.us

National Council of La Raza (NCLR)—The largest national Hispanic civil rights and advocacy organization in the United States, NCLR addresses many issues, including early childhood education. The organization's website features research, reports, and resources, including a 2012 Dual Language Learner Teacher Competencies Report. www.nclr.org

World-Class Instructional Design and Assessment—WIDA advances academic language development and academic achievement for linguistically diverse students through high-quality standards, assessments, research, and professional development for educators. The Early Language Development Standards aim to provide developmentally appropriate suggestions for supporting, teaching, and assessing dual language learners. The website includes free webinars and resource guides. www.wida.us/standards/EarlyYears.aspx

Children's Book Resources

Finding and selecting books that engage dual language learners and represent their cultures and languages can be challenging. Look for books that focus on concepts that are meaningful to young children and provide a platform for storytelling and project-based learning activities, such as the Around the World series, by Ann Morris (Harper Collins). Other books provide interesting information in many different languages, such as the beautifully illustrated *Little Treasures: Endearments From Around the World*, written by Jacqueline K. Ogburn and illustrated by Chris Raschka (Houghton Mifflin Harcourt 2011). This book provides a wonderful conversation starter about the language families use to express love and tenderness in different cultures. The resources in this section offer guidance for locating and using a variety of books to support young DLLs.

The Head Start's National Center on Cultural and Linguistic Responsiveness offers two sets of guidelines for selecting books.

- Selecting and Using Culturally Responsive Children's Books: www.eclkc.ohs.acf.hhs.gov/hslc/tta-system/cultural-linguistic/docs/selecting-culturally-appropriate-books.pdf

- Quick Guide for Teachers—How to Use Bilingual Books: www.eclkc.ohs.acf.hhs.gov/hslc/tta-system/cultural-linguistic/docs/ncclr-qguide-how-to-use-bilingual-books.pdf

The following websites recommend, recognize, or publish outstanding books for young children.

- Día! Diversity in Action
  http://dia.ala.org

- Pura Belpré Award
  www.ala.org/alsc/awardsgrants/bookmedia/belpremedal

- Children's Literature and Reading Special Interest Group of the International Reading Association
  http://clrsig.org/index.php

- Lee & Low Books
  www.leeandlow.com

- Language Lizard Books
  www.languagelizard.com

- Star Bright Books
  www.starbrightbooks.org

- East West Discovery Press
  www.eastwestdiscovery.com

- Cinco Puntos Press
  www.cincopuntos.com

- Me + Mi Publishing
  www.memima.com

- Culture for Kids
  www.cultureforkids.com

Reflecting, Discussing, and Exploring
Questions and Follow-Up Activities

Karen N. Nemeth

The articles in *Spotlight on Young Children: Supporting Dual Language Learners* provide guidance for early childhood educators who work with children who are learning two or more languages. With the growing diversity of children and families served by early childhood programs, and research and policies about how best to support dual language learners continually evolving, it is crucial for all early childhood educators to remain current in their knowledge and skills. Examining your current beliefs and practices is an important first step in this process. The research-based, classroom-tested strategies in this book will help you adapt your curriculum, environment, and practices to support each child's home language and culture as well as their learning of a new language.

To help readers review and expand on ideas, we have developed this study guide—a series of questions and follow-up activities. First, we invite you to think about your own early experiences with languages. We then ask you to make connections between your early experiences and strategies for promoting children's dual language learning. Specific questions and suggested activities related to each article then follow. Finally, general questions about curriculum, teaching practices, resources, and next steps can help you pull together concepts and teaching strategies.

A. Recalling Your Own Early Experiences

1. Think about your own language development experiences. Are you fluent in more than one language? Are you able to speak some words or phrases in an additional language? Do you recall childhood friends, neighbors, or extended family members who spoke other languages? If you grew up speaking more than one language, what do you recall about your early language and literacy experiences in school? What were the challenges? What ex-

periences were most beneficial? Have you ever been in a situation in which people spoke a language you did not understand? How did this make you feel?

2. What early experiences do you recall with other cultures? How did you learn about different languages? How do you celebrate your own culture? How would you describe your culture to someone you have recently met? What elements do you think should be considered part of your culture?

3. What languages did you grow up hearing in your community? What languages do you hear around you as an adult? How have the languages and cultures you encounter in your work changed over time? What do you wish you knew about these languages and cultures?

B. Expanding on Each Article

"Creating Supportive Caregiving Environments for Infant and Toddler Dual Language Learners"/ Rebecca Parlakian and Jennifer Frey

This article describes ways infant and toddler teachers can support young dual language learners' emerging language and literacy skills. It suggests five areas in which programs can provide high-quality language environments to support infants and toddlers and their families.

1. Discuss with a partner the ways your program staff build relationships with children's families. How do staff communicate with families who speak a home language other than English? In the section "Relationship Building and Engaging With Families," review the questions that invite families to share background information. How many of these questions does your program already ask on forms or during home visits? Which questions could you add to give staff a more complete understanding of individual families?

2. Some families may believe that their children

should hear just one language in order to learn it, and that they might be confused if they are also hearing another language. Using some of the research and ideas from this article, how can you explain to families the benefits and importance of helping children learn two or more languages simultaneously rather than focusing on one language?

3. Physical cues can support very young dual language learners' full participation in the program. With your eyes closed, mentally list the materials in your setting that reflect children's home languages and cultures. How many can you remember? Do you think you remembered all of the materials or just some? Where are these items in the setting (within children's reach, used as decorations on the walls)? Next, open your eyes and walk through your setting, noting the materials that reflect the children's home languages and cultures. Be sure to look at the materials from children's eye level. Identify each one, how it can be used, and where it is located in the environment. Finally, review your list and identify new materials you could add that reflect families' languages and cultures and that the children in your program would enjoy.

"Enhancing Practice With Infants and Toddlers From Diverse Language and Cultural Backgrounds" / Karen N. Nemeth and Valeria Erdosi

It is important for infants and toddlers to see and hear their home languages and cultures represented in the program. Nemeth and Erdosi share examples from a diverse infant/toddler program and discuss the research and recommendations behind the suggested strategies.

4. If you were about to enroll your child in an infant/toddler program in another country, think about what you would want the teachers to know about your family's background. In what way would you prefer to give teachers this information? How can you learn more about the cultural and linguistic backgrounds of the infants and toddlers in your own program?

5. What kinds of activities can you invite families to participate in that will help them feel more engaged in their child's early learning program? How can you discover more about the talents, knowledge, and assets families can contribute to your program?

6. How does representing each child's language and culture in the classroom benefit all children? How can visible representations of the families' languages and cultures also encourage more family engagement?

"Many Languages, One Teacher: Supporting Language and Literacy Development for Dual Language Learners" / Elizabeth S. Magruder, Whitcomb W. Hayslip, Linda M. Espinosa, and Carola Matera

The authors describe the challenges of meeting the diverse language needs of preschoolers and provide evidence-based strategies for meeting those needs in multilingual preschool classrooms. The Personalized Oral Language(s) Learning program offers intentional plans and techniques for teachers to provide targeted attention to children's learning of their home languages and English.

7. As the authors note, children's oral language skills are critical not only to their communication with others but also to their reading development. How does learning more than one language at the same time both benefit and create challenges for young children?

8. What environmental supports does this article recommend to enhance children's language development and learning in general? What kinds of materials and displays are important, and where can you obtain them? How many of these supports does your setting already provide? Which ones could you try implementing tomorrow or next week?

9. The article describes six instructional supports. Describe the supports you might use in your program. What would you need to implement them? How can you intentionally address the needs of DLLs with these instructional supports?

"Learning in English, Learning in Spanish: A Head Start Program Changes Its Approach" / Joan Youngquist and Bárbara Martínez-Griego

This article details one Head Start program's journey to change the way they teach dual language learners, who lagged behind their peers in language skills after one year in the program. The staff and administrators examined their policies and practices, and through intentional collaboration they made significant changes that resulted in similar language and literacy skill levels between DLLs and their peers.

10. Think of an early learning program with which you are familiar. How does this program support dual language learners? How does it support the home languages and cultures of the children and their families? Imagine if this program wanted to become a dual language program, as described in this article. What would be the biggest obstacle to implementing a dual-language approach in this setting? What would be the program's greatest asset?

11. In Step 2 of the process to transform the program's approach to language and learning, the authors describe challenges the staff experienced. Think of a time when you experimented with a different approach in your teaching. What inspired you to try something new? How did your expected outcomes compare with the actual outcomes? What did you learn from that experience?

12. Why is having a strong foundation in their home languages essential to children's learning success? What challenges arise in supporting children's home languages when teachers speak only English? How can administrators help teachers in this situation?

"Supporting Dual Language Learners With Challenging Behaviors" / Karen N. Nemeth and Pamela Brillante

Finding solutions to challenging behaviors when a child and teacher speak different languages can be difficult. Suggestions in this article focus on prevention, observation, and specialized strategies that any early childhood educator can use effectively.

13. Think of a child's behavior that presented challenges you were not able to resolve easily. Have you encountered this issue with a child who didn't speak your language? What are some key factors that indicate whether a child's behavior is likely due to language differences or to other reasons?

14. Evaluate your setting for ways it might be stressful for young DLLs. What could you change in the environment to prevent language barriers from leading a child to use challenging behaviors?

"Engaging Dual Language Learners in Projects" / Meredith K. Jones and Pamela L. Shue

Working together on in-depth projects gives all children hands-on experiences that help them overcome language barriers, build vocabulary, and develop social skills. The project described in this article provides a real-world context for children's learning and for engaging families as well.

15. The author introduces a teacher-initiated project that would be familiar to most young children—pizza. What projects or topics would appeal to and be familiar to most of the children in your program? Describe a project—teacher initiated or child initiated—you found to be particularly successful with young children. Why was it so successful? What features of the project approach made it especially effective for children who are DLLs?

16. How did the teacher in the article introduce the project topic to the dual language learners? What strategies can you adopt from the article to prepare dual language learners when starting a new project?

17. Describe ways the teacher involved the children's families in the project. How did she connect with families whose home language was Spanish? How does involving families in projects benefit the teachers, the children, and the families? In your next project, what strategies can you use to involve families who speak different languages?

"Where's Your Partner? Pairing Bilingual Learners in Dual Language Classrooms" / Iliana Alanís

Helping young children learn together in bilingual pairs gives them opportunities to practice oral language and social interaction skills in a supportive environment. This is an effective way to validate home languages and make all children feel that they have something valuable to contribute to the classroom.

18. When you take a step back and let children interact with each other as part of their learning experience, this means you believe they have something important to say. Reflect on your teaching practice. What might you change or adjust to give children more opportunities for meaningful interaction?

19. Children often require explicit modeling and practice before they can start partner work. Think about the different situations children might face when they work in pairs. How can you help them understand the expectations for paired learning and prepare them for a successful learning experience with their partners? How might you prepare them for issues that may arise?

20. When you invite children to work in pairs, how do you encourage them to discuss the activity with their partner? Sentence stems, such as *In my opinion . . .* or *I noticed . . .*, provide a structure for children's language development and help them organize their thoughts and feelings. Develop four stems for children to use when learning with a partner. Post them where children can see them easily and practice using them regularly.

"Using Technology as a Teaching Tool for Dual Language Learners" / Karen N. Nemeth and Fran S. Simon

This article presents a broad array of technology-based solutions for teaching dual language learners in prekindergarten through third grade. The authors describe how technology can help teachers adapt current materials, make connections to each child's language and culture, and encourage DLLs to demonstrate their knowledge and skills.

21. What forms of technology do you use in your program? How do you use the Internet, software, or apps to help you connect with dual language learners and their families and provide information in their home languages? What technology do you wish you could have to better meet the diverse language needs in your classroom?

22. Read "Technology and Interactive Media as Tools in Early Childhood Programs Serving Children From Birth Through Age 8," a joint position statement issued by NAEYC and the Fred Rogers Center for Early Learning and Children's Media at Saint Vincent College, available at www.naeyc.org/content/technology-and-young-children. How does the technology position statement specifically address the learning needs of dual language learners? How might that guidance be included in your program or school policies and shared with families?

23. What are some ways you can use technology to adapt early learning activities and materials you already have and use them effectively with dual language learners? How can technology devices help young DLLs show what they know and can do?

"Integrating Content and Mechanics in New Language Learners' Writing" / Daniel R. Meier

When children in the primary grades are learning a new language, they need specialized supports for linking oral and written language. The author focuses on techniques to support the integration of content and mechanics of writing for dual language learners in kindergarten through third grade.

24. What challenges in written language mechanics affect dual language learners, as described in the article? Which of these challenges—and what others—have you encountered in your work with children? How have you addressed these challenges?

25. Explain to a partner the importance of content in terms of writing development and the basic mechanics of writing. What is the relationship between content learning and writing mechanics when DLLs are learning to write?

26. What learning activities do you use to support the development of children's writing skills? Consider some strategies that are commonly used in primary classrooms, such as sentence frames and read-alouds of the children's writings. How could you adapt those strategies for dual language learners? How could you modify the strategies for use with DLLs in kindergarten and first grade?

"Principles of a Dual Language Learner Program" / Paula Moujalli, Laura Haim, and Ryan W. Pontier

The authors describe how they successfully manage a dual language program for infants, toddlers, and preschoolers. With explanations of the research behind their practices, they offer a series of guiding principles for administrators or directors who are considering implementing a dual language program or who would like to better support dual language learners and their families.

27. The article opens with a vignette about code switching, where a young child uses both Spanish and English to express himself. Think of the dual language learners in your program. Have you heard them use words from more than one language in the same sentence? Have you heard adults do this? With a partner, talk about the benefits of code switching and ways teachers can support children when they use this way of communicating.

28. Leadership is a critical component of the dual language program's success. Make a list of the ways the administrators in this program provide leadership to staff, children, and families. How do the administrators in your program offer good leadership? How do you serve as a leader for the children and families you work with? Consider ideas from the article that might help you become a more effective leader.

29. In this article the administrators describe ways they support teachers in their program. Consider the professional development opportunities discussed in the article. How would the teachers you work with benefit from similar opportunities? What additional experiences might help them grow professionally? How could you include these experiences in existing professional development workshops or classes?

C. Making Connections

Consider the Big Picture

1. In your view, what are the three main themes or take-away messages in this collection of articles? Discuss your ideas with others to find commonalities and unique impressions. As a group, pick three key messages that you can make the focus of changes in your program.

2. The articles in this book note the interconnectedness of language and culture. Many experts suggest that because all language is rooted in culture, support for dual language learners should involve not just vocabulary but also the cultural contexts of language and literacy development. After reading this book, what insights have you gained about the relationship between culture and language? Why is it important to incorporate children's cultures and languages into the curriculum? How can you better understand each child's cultural background?

3. All articles in this collection include ideas for building vocabulary in children's first and second languages. Review the strategies found in the articles and compile a list of those that will work in your classroom.

4. Research and observations show that dual language learners experience language benefits when they interact with their peers and with adults. Explore the ways interpersonal conversations benefit the children in your program by recording children's significant discussions with each other or with you. Note the topic and any snippets of conversation you think are important. Next, examine your notes. Are there differences in the amount of time monolingual and bilingual children speak with each other or with you? Which strategies from this book could you use to enhance children's conversations, especially those of dual language learners?

Examine Curriculum Goals and Expected Outcomes

5. Review NAEYC's position statement titled "Responding to Linguistic and Cultural Diversity: Recommendations for Effective Early Childhood Education" (1995), which stresses the importance of valuing the home languages and cultures of dual language learners. (Access this document at www.naeyc.org/positionstatements/linguistic.) Select three quotes from the position statement to discuss with a group of colleagues or peers. How does the position statement support what you learned from the articles in this collection? How do your program practices align with NAEYC's position statement? What could you do differently to better support NAEYC's recommendations?

6. How does the content of the articles relate to the curriculum your program uses? How does your curriculum provide for the needs of dual language learners—for example, are materials and lesson plans available in languages other than English? Are they available in *every* language needed in your classroom? Several articles discuss how teachers intentionally adapted lesson plans to meet the needs of dual language learners. Using some sample lesson plans, work with your colleagues to describe adaptations that would meet the needs of specific dual language learners in your setting.

Use Reflection to Enhance Teaching Practices

7. Which ideas presented in the articles or raised in your discussions affirm your work with or on behalf of young children and their families, especially dual language learners? Which ideas cause you to question your practices? What practices might you need to change to better serve diverse families? List at least three changes you plan to make as a result of reading this collection of articles. Then discuss these ideas with your group to compare and contrast your responses. What new approaches might you use to promote DLLs' learning? How do you think these changes would benefit children and families?

8. Several articles presented the idea of using observations and gathering examples of children's language skills and other knowledge in both English and their home languages. It can be difficult to find assessment tools that evaulate children's knowledge of non-English languages. What new approaches did you learn to help children show what they know and can do in any language?

Focus on Families and Communities

9. Many of the articles in this collection discuss family involvement and engagement. What three ideas did you discover that would help improve your partnerships with families who speak different languages? With a colleague or peer, share an example of a challenge you faced in relating to a family. Discuss new strategies you learned from this book that might enable you to have more successful interactions in the future.

10. Consider how to convey to families the importance of supporting home language and literacy outside of their children's program. What five activities did you learn in this book that you can share with families to help them build their children's skills in their home languages? What resources would you need to support those activities? Review the resources starting on page 87 and select several that you think would be most useful for the families in your program. How can you make these available and accessible to them?

Identify Resources and Plan Next Steps

11. Review the extensive resource list provided in this book (starting on p. 87). Make a note of the items you have read and found useful, and share these with your colleagues or peers. Create a new list for yourself of additional resources that others recommend to you.

12. With others, choose one article or book and one online resource that none of you has used. Make plans to read or review these resources and meet later to discuss your reactions and ways to implement what you learned.

13. Use one of the resources on page 91 to locate a children's book that supports dual language learners—perhaps a storybook in children's home language or a book that introduces children to simple words in several languages or to other cultures. With your colleagues or peers, discuss your reactions to the book and how it might support learning in your diverse classroom. Work together to create a lesson plan or project based on the book. What languages do the children in your classroom speak that are not supported by the book? In what ways could you adapt the book to meet their needs? Identify materials and resources that would support the learning activity you have planned.

14. Researchers, experts, and educators agree that the early childhood field still has much to do to address *all* children's needs and to help each child learn and thrive. What questions do you still have after reading these articles and completing the professional learning tasks? Create a plan of action for your own professional development, including what resources you need, where you can find them, and what you want to accomplish in your teaching practice.

CPSIA information can be obtained
at www.ICGtesting.com
Printed in the USA
JSHW041426261121
20754JS00002B/2

9 781938 113130